The Romance Trap

ROMANCE TRAP

PEG GRYMES

BRANDON

First published in 1996 by
Brandon Book Publishers Ltd
Dingle, Co. Kerry, Ireland

Copyright © Peg Grymes 1996

The moral rights of the author have been asserted.

British Library Cataloguing-in-Publication Data is available for
this book.

ISBN 0 86322 219 6

Front cover painting, "The Tree of Forgiveness" by Edward
Burne Jones. Reproduced by kind permission of the Board of
Trustees of the National Museums and Galleries on Mersyside
(Lady Lever Art Gallery, Port Sunlight)

Cover design by the Public Communications Centre, Dublin
Typeset by Koinonia Ltd, Bury
Printed by Colour Books, Dublin

Contents

❧

Acknowledgements

Thanks to my mother, Mary Buckley, who taught me about love. Thanks to Liam, Colm and Lochlan: with them, family continues to be the place where I find my most important thoughts. And thanks to all of our extended family for not only providing emotional support, but a very stimulating intellectual environment as well.

Thank you to the many writers and artists who tell their own personal stories and touch many lives. With their help, I find inspiration to work and aspiration to love in the same place.

A very important note of thanks to Mary Maher of *The Irish Times*, who helped shape this book, to my editor at Brandon, Peter Malone, and publisher Steve MacDonogh, and to Winifred Power.

Introduction

❧

While many books are written about love and romance, few address romance as a social construction, an elaborate arrangement of sexualised gender relations. We are not accustomed to thinking of romance in quite this way. It is so much a part of our world, almost like the air we breathe, that we rarely think of it as an invention of our own making.

We may be enchanted or disenchanted by the world of romance, but we are hardly ever really analytical and critical. Though there has been considerable emphasis on the nature of marriage and the nuclear family in feminist theory, there has been very little reflection on the deep-seated romantic ideals and illusions that continue to appeal to most women.[1] This gap in our thinking has created opportunities for conservatives and anti-feminists to argue that feminism is primarily defensive, anti-men and anti-sex. Meanwhile, self-help and self-therapy books have stepped into the vacuum created by the absence of enlightened feminist perspectives, offering advice and counsel to the many women who love too much, love the wrong kinds of men, or are inordinately grateful for being loved at all.

This is a political book, but it has been written as a result of personal experience. As I began to put my thoughts and feelings into writing, I still felt emotional about some of my recollections. I must admit that at times I thought about writing under a pseudonym and even thought of trying to turn all of this into some kind of fiction, but to treat ourselves as characters and the fabric of our lives as "episodes" is a dangerous temptation. Women have lived at one remove from themselves for long enough.

These pages, which are about me, are infused with the knowledge of two generations of feminism, giving way to a third. It took an intellectual appreciation of feminism's first two waves, coupled with a critical personal crisis, for me to embrace myself and a form of feminism which is not only structural and political, but relevant in the most personal way – in the interior world of the self.

Perhaps we have become too accustomed to the "big themes" of structural, sociological and political analyses to believe that matters of personal relationships can be of interest and relevance to political development. Our impulse is to dismiss personal experience and the knowledge we gain from it as "anecdotal". We discredit personal knowledge for being self-concerned and subjective. Yet our own experiences are our only source of reference and inspiration. Feminist writer and poet Adrienne Rich realised this, and emphasised the need for all women to speak truthfully to one another about their experiences, for "we have a profound stake, beyond the personal, in the project of describing our reality as candidly and fully as we can".[2]

The personal world is not in contrast or opposition to social life, but is the basic unit of collective experience. As I began to share the truth of my life with other women, I started to understand that our most personal truths take us beyond the "merely personal". When I tell my secrets and blunders, I realise my mistakes are not simply mistakes and neither are they simply mine. In this book, I describe events that are not particularly unique experiences – and a person who is not a special kind of woman.

Our individual traumas reflect universal ones. As a woman, I lived a phenomenon of responding to my own discontent by projecting my needs and aspirations onto other people, hoping I could find satisfaction through them. Now I can see the ridiculousness and desperation of the pattern I fulfilled. But only through the most personal analyses – by talking and listening to the stories of other women – have I begun to understand the degree to which we have tended to privatise our problems and have failed to see the details of our "personal" traumas and "mistakes" in the patterns of a more vast, collective predicament.

Recently, feminist activist Gloria Steinem wrote that she has begun to "learn from other women, to figure out the politics of my own life, and to experiment with telling the truth in public".[3] I have also found that the diagnosis of a wider struggle begins with telling and listening to the truth of women's narrative. In this, every woman may be an instrument for the consciousness of others, as we realise that in each of our personal dramas we live the lives of many women. So I do not hesitate to reveal my thoughts and experiences to you. The personal ceases to be personal now. I offer it to you, in the hope that as I write of my illusions of the romantic world I am contributing to our awareness, not mine alone.

The Culture of Romance

WOMEN SPEND A lot of time preparing for, and recovering from, romantic involvements. Though we may sometimes feel uncertain, confused, even cynical, we still devote an enormous amount of our energy and attention to our boyfriends, lovers or partners. At times romance seems to consume us. The cover of any women's magazine you see on the newsstands suggests that women are preoccupied with men and how to attract them. We spend endless hours watching romantic comedies, romantic dramas, romantic tragedies. We have kept an industry afloat with our demand for romantic novels depicting men with chiselled features and women with billowing skirts on the jacket.

Many feminists are confounded, even angered by women's preoccupation with romance. But it may be that all these far-fetched tales of noble deeds and romantic quests, of personal sacrifices and faithfulness unto death, contain a profound reality. Many women do believe that romantic involvement is the supreme human experience, the closest we come to wholeness, completion, fulfilment. When we are in love, life is more meaningful. We feel, somehow, more alive.

Philosopher Robert Johnson writes, "In the aspirations of romantic love there is a deep psychological truth that reverberates in our souls, that awakens us to what we are at our best, what we are when we are whole. No one can be unmoved [by romance], unless he be made of ice, for in these loves, adventures, and acts of devotion, there is revealed all that is noble, loving, faithful, and most high within our own selves." And he suggests that, in Western cultures, romance has "supplanted religion as the arena in which... women seek meaning, transcendence, wholeness, and ecstasy."[1]

And so it is difficult to look dispassionately at matters of romance. We are afraid that we might drive out love, happiness, fulfilment. We fear that life will be cold and unexciting. And yet, if we are honest with ourselves, we must admit that the romantic approach to love is not working very well. If we consider our own romantic pasts and look at the people around us, we see that romance doesn't often translate into a sustained love or commitment.

I believe that it is possible to distinguish profound human love from the culture of romance, and that profound love can only be realised when it is freed from romantic beliefs. In examining romance, I do not want to destroy love but to understand it better, to explore it as an experience and a kind of sharing that takes us beyond ourselves, and to show that this has little to do with the extreme and elusive qualities of the romantic model that we have inherited. The challenge for women, and for men, is to look "not only at the beauty and potential in romantic love but also at the contradictions and illusions we carry around inside us at the unconscious level."[2]

We have all imbibed the potion and have all been drunk on it. But whether we enjoy it or not, approve of it or not, take part in it wholeheartedly or not, the question for feminists must be: what role does the culture of romance play in the politics of patriarchy? How have the unconscious contradictions and illusions which women carry within themselves affected our lives?

Feminist writer and poet Adrienne Rich argues that there is a great deal of social pressure on women to look to men to fulfil their emotional and sexual needs. Insofar as this is true, Rich argues that our orientation toward romantic love is not "natural", but is a culturally constructed version of gender relations and sexuality. She also suggests that women's involvement in the world of romance reduces their identification with their own intrinsic interests. Attachments to men, she argues, seem to affect women's ways of thinking, not only thinking about their work and their economic future, but also thinking about their roles as whole, varied people, viable in themselves.[3]

Up to this point feminism has relied heavily – probably too heavily – on the importance of paid work outside the home to resolve women's dependence on men. Perhaps the thought of becoming financially independent of men seemed to promise that other forms of independence would follow. But we may have underestimated the resilience of romantic ideals and the unlikelihood of their simply falling away. "There is something awesome in these huge, culturally transmitted systems of belief... It is as though we breathed them in from novels and movies, from the psychological air around us, and they became part of us, as though fused with the cells of our bodies. We all know we are supposed to 'fall in love' and that our relationships must be based on romance."[4]

It is not easy to leave behind all of the grand stories, fairy tales and images of women and men, and how we are supposed to relate to one another. These have been our cultural staples, the stuff out of which we have constructed images of ourselves and imaginings of our futures. In our everyday conversation, we use the word "romance" to refer to almost any attraction between two people. If a couple is having a sexual liaison, people say they are romantically involved. If two people love each other and persevere together, we consider theirs a great romance. The fact that we say "romance" when we mean "love" suggests a kind of psychological muddle in which we have lost our understanding of both and the differences between them. This is part of the reason why a feminist enquiry into how men and women might relate to each other is so important. What starts here as an exploration into the meaning of romance leads to more searching questions about the possibilities of achieving love between equals.

In one of the few studies of Western romance as a social and cultural construction, anthropologists Dorothy Holland and Margaret Skinner studied university students at the time that women of my age were at university. They described an ideal model of modern romance, where a man and a woman who are attracted to one another learn of each other's qualities and uniqueness as people. The relationship provides intimacy, both emotional and physical.[5]

A central feature of this romantic culture is the idea of a mutually favourable exchange. Philosopher Erich Fromm noted that "For the man an attractive girl – and for the woman an attractive man – are the prizes they are after. 'Attractive' usually means a nice package of qualities which are popular and sought after on the personality market. What specifically makes a person attractive depends on the fashion of the time."[6]

And so these cultural models not only describe a sequence of events that may lead to the establishment of an intimate relationship or marriage, but also place sexual relations within a "calculus of attractiveness" in which sexual attraction is the commodity of value in an ongoing sexual marketplace. According to these criteria, accomplished or good-looking men are often thought to "deserve" good-looking women.

Although romantic culture may seem to place men and women on an equal footing, with different though equally valuable qualities and experiences to offer one another, closer examination reveals a different, more traditional picture. Women have no real choice as to whether they want to put themselves forward as players on the romantic scene or not, and often find themselves judged at inappropriate times and by inappropriate people – in other words, when they have not wanted to be looked upon in a sexualised way. In the world of romance, men are in the position of judging; women are exposed to having their behaviour interpreted.

Holland and Eisenhart found that women's goals, intentions and qualities were likely to be assessed by others according to a range of romantic types. Young women were cast by their friends and acquaintances as actors in the romantic world, sometimes in the most inappropriate circumstances. One student was embarrassed and offended by being viewed romantically "by men [like her professor] whom she considered inappropriate partners".[7] Many others experienced incidents in which they "could not prevent themselves from being evaluated for their sexual attractiveness". While some of the students believed that romantic and sexual issues would become relevant if and only if they wanted them to, others were beginning to realise that they were always vulnerable to being judged and valued primarily in terms of sexual attractiveness.

Yet despite our qualms and unease, most of us continue to care and worry about interpretations of ourselves as romantic types. Like the women in this study, we regard romance as a natural activity that most people engage in, and engage in at a reasonable level of competence. Holland and Eisenhart found that no one talked of romance and romantic relationships as something at which one was good or bad, expert or inexpert. "Knowledge of romantic relationships and interest in them was largely taken for granted."[8]

We are continually supplied with interpretations of ourselves as romantic types. We might not always be explicitly aware of the signposts that guide our interactions – we focus our attention on the topic of conversation, not on the social symbolism underlying our speech, gestures and dress – but we approach one another and bond according to social cues. All the while we are constructing our own definitions of what is romantic or attractive. One of the women in Holland and

Eisenhart's study talked about how she would like to be more attractive: "[When I am with my girlfriends] we always talk about our boyfriends, or how fat we are – we all say that... None of us have to lose weight, but we just want to be thinner... I'm gonna lose weight and clear up my face and grow my hair out, so I'll be all beautiful this summer."[9]

The scene was much the same at my university. Being at an élite school, surrounded by thousands of gifted and talented women, did not exempt us from playing the usual, distorted roles in the game of attraction.

I remember one particular day, I was running a bit later than usual and, for reasons having to do with scheduling and location I planned to eat at the undergraduates' dining-hall. But first I needed to make my way to the women's bathroom, urgently. Got there, pushed the door. Nothing. Pushed the door again. Still nothing. A porter happened to be passing by, and I asked him if he was in the midst of cleaning and if he would be finished soon. No, he explained, the door to the women's bathroom was locked at mealtimes.

I wondered if there was some kind of misunderstanding. Maybe I hadn't heard him right. So I went out of my way to get back to that hall on other evenings, and each time I returned the door was still locked. It seems that too many women were purging themselves of the meals they had just eaten to allow things go on as they had. Perhaps they were disturbing the plumbing. Solution? Lock the door to the women's toilets.

So women can now attend Yale, an impossible thing only a couple of decades ago. We can be amongst the "best and the brightest". We can reach the heights of corporate success. If many of us still suffer from an inner illness or a deep self-loathing, now we can do that at Yale.

To see and know women who are beautiful in their uniqueness, who are intelligent and gifted in numerous ways, and then discover a deep, secret sickness of self, is jolting. It's a contradiction that forces us to realise that politics and policies alone have not solved the problems which continue to diminish our lives.

But we really cannot consider it too surprising that the the world of romance and attractiveness looms so large in the lives of young women, even to a degree that is sometimes fatal. "Spending time and money to make oneself physically attractive, to hear from others about romantic endeavours, to plan for activities in which romantic possibilities can be exercised, and even to give up on one's own interests, activities or plans, all make sense when viewed from the perspective of the model of romantic relationships and the route to prestige it prescribes for women."[10]

Holland and Eisenhart found that for those young women looking for "Mr Right" – or at least someone they liked enough to go out with – there was often a temptation to form a long-term relationship in order to escape the uncomfortable aspects of being on the "sexual auction block", as Holland and Eisenhart termed it. No doubt there are men who also follow this impulse into serious relationships because they are uncomfortable with their own roles in this scheme, and are just as anxious to remove themselves from it. While most of the students generally accepted the emphasis on romance and spent much time and energy responding to it, some of the women devised ways to circumvent aspects of the system.

Susan, who was uncomfortable with the whole idea of romantic involvement, managed to keep romantic possibilities at bay for some time by talking about her boyfriend a lot, though she rarely made plans to meet him and he never appeared on her campus. Others, perhaps equally uncomfortable but less resourceful, simply gave over wholly to romantic stereotypes. One newcomer to a dorm, having been teased by a group of female dorm-mates for being a virgin, transformed herself into a "good-time girl". The other women's urgings and innu-endos amounted to a kind of pressure and encouragement to which the newcomer, eager to be accepted by her friends, succumbed entirely.

Of those uncomfortable with the world of romance, some found an uneasy refuge in acquiescence. Others found ways of avoiding the issue, keeping up appearances without actually forming significant romantic attachments. Yet others tried to handle their misgivings by keeping opportunities for romance at bay. For those who tried this tactic, the objective was usually to balance the demands of a romantic relationship with other interests, like school or sports, but this stance usually cost the women dearly in terms of prestige.

More serious challenges to traditional romantic culture were hard to come by. Some spoke of the discrepancy between their feelings and their actions, but only a few revealed truly oppositional or heretical views about romance. Just one explicitly criticised the idea that a boyfriend should be a source of prestige. Even when they felt that they were mistreated in relationships, a sense of acquiescence prevailed. One woman who had problems in her romance saw it as her responsibility to get her boyfriend to treat her better.

In general, these women did not view their grievances as "women's issues" but as matters of choosing and managing their own lifestyles. Their only resistance to romantic culture amounted to a variety of forms of "dodging the system". More direct challenges to the system are hard to muster, partly because in the politics of romance, the exact source of authority and standards of gender relations is pretty vague. In the study discussed here, the student community did share a sense that there was a dominant or prevailing perspective on attractiveness and on relationships between men and women, but the actual arbitrators of attractiveness and attraction varied according to circumstances. The judges may be the guys who came to a particular party, or the cute one who sits in the next row in class, or the other women in the dorm. Those who feel offended or oppressed by romantic standards have no clear source of authority to criticise.

With no real authority to blame, we tend to see our grievances as individual problems. More than that, the young women Holland and Eisenhart studied "did not really believe that gender discrimination affected them personally in any systematic way"; those who did "felt that they were clever enough as individuals to circumvent it when they encountered it".

When we are very young women, still imagining ourselves invulnerable and still confident of our ability to avoid the hazards before us, the world of patriarchy and male privilege may seem unrelated to our experience and our challenges to the system may be extremely limited. We each view ourselves as the magnificent exception, the one who will rise above it all.

When I was making my own transitions from girlhood to womanhood, I could never have imagined the experiences and insights the future held. Anytime I picked up a book or article about a woman who had failed to live according to her own will or had failed to live her own authentic experience, I thought, "But that's not about me. I'm different." Yet when social scientist Sharon Thompson studied women of my generation when we were teenagers, she found that despite the accomplishments of the women's movement, we continued to cling rather conventionally to notions of men bringing definition and purpose to our lives. Girls of my generation still expected romance and sex to form our "fundamental projects" and experiences. Despite the instability of the nuclear family, the incidence of divorce and abandonment, and the disruption many of our own families had experienced, we continued to value relationships in terms of the romantic ideals of "true love, permanence, and monogamy".[11] We have grown to become – or will fail to become – the feminists of the twenty-first century.

Not many years ago I was still at university, still single and focused on my own intentions, still feeling the exception to any rule. Though the university I attended had begun to admit women undergraduates only a little more than a decade before I arrived, I felt no hardship. When I was there, I did not feel the anger that frustration with concrete, legal barriers brought to the women of the '60s and '70s. I had been pretty well rewarded for my efforts. Having graduated from Berkeley, I was offered a scholarship to study further at Yale. It would have been hard for me not to have had a certain amount of faith in the old adage about "hard work and determination" being the only requirements for success. I was getting my piece of the pie. I was basically content with my status and progress.

I even felt a subversive kind of satisfaction in my presence at an Ivy League bastion of male privilege. On my way to classes I would walk past the all-male, white, Protestant secret societies' meeting houses and feel superior to these anachronisms. As I passed the crumbling tombs of the old privileged graveyard, I would often read the cast-iron promise on its gates: "Eternal glory to those who enter these hallowed grounds." I pitied the desperate souls who searched for salvation in a New Haven mausoleum.

But what will be the lot and legacy of the women of my generation, now able to tread upon the old patriarchs? It would seem that we should be in the best position to benefit from the work of the women's movement. Thanks to feminists who came before us, conditions for women really are different from what they were just a short while ago. The protection of the Civil Rights Act was extended to women in the USA in 1964, when I was a new baby. Before I was ten years old, the Equal Rights Amendment, which would remove all legal, economic and social restrictions on women, was passed by the US Congress and sent to the individual state senates for ratification. Before I was twenty, thirty-five states had passed that amendment.

Throughout the world the women's rights movement has made significant progress. In more than 90 per cent of the world's nations, women can vote and hold public office. And while complete political, economic and social equality remains to be achieved, the United Nations Commission on the Status of Women has helped women in many nations gain legal rights and fuller access to education and professions.

It would seem that women of my generation should be confident as we walk through this world – no longer a "man's world" but one that is ours as well. But in the more than twenty years since the women's movement began in earnest, we have continued to see women suffer from an intense insecurity, a subtle suffering, often expressed and reflected in deeply unhappy relationships with men.

Whatever we may have accomplished in legislation, the gap between women's and men's understanding of relationship, marriage and home life has remained wide. For many women, relationships are the centre of our universe, often to a fault. We tend to subordinate ourselves and our work to our relationships. We depend on them, and they on us, so much that we may expect the relationships in our lives to define life itself. Certainly we are entitled to our desire for emotional intimacy, but even those men who do their best to live up to our expectations may wonder how and why they are supposed to lend us the definition we really should find for ourselves. To complicate things further, many women simultaneously look to men for this definition and resent them for seeming to hold the power to define us.

Most women hope to find intimacy and companionship in their relationships, yet, across classes and cultures, we have not been finding these qualities in men.[12] If our needs have seemed fairly simple or basic to us, they have never seemed simple to men. Many men have felt bewildered by what seem to be new, changing, increasing demands for intimacy and have felt ill-prepared to meet these new standards.[13]

Some of our mutual bewilderment and dissatisfaction may have to do with the fact that men and women come to relationships from different perspectives. Psychotherapist Anne Wilson Schaef writes that for men "the center of the universe is the self and work. Everything else must go through, relate to, and be defined by the self and the work. Other things in life may be important (relationships, spirituality, hobbies, and so forth), but they are never of equal importance; they always occupy positions on the periphery of the man's life, on the outside circle."[14]

Now, as ever, many women feel unable to coax or cajole their husbands into greater modes of involvement in their relationship. So we get used to it. Many of us come to expect that we will give men more attention and affection than we receive from them. We cease to expect true reciprocity and mutual support. Many women fall into a kind of compassion trap, where we find ourselves expected to provide emotional support and encouragement for our partners, even to the extent of subordinating our own needs as individuals. The notion that such matters are private only contributes to many women's sense of isolation and resignation to their roles.[15]

The heavy burden of such relationships is bound to exact a toll, perhaps best measured by the anxieties and disappointments of women in marriage. Sociologist Jessie Bernard identifies a kind of "dual experience of marriage" – two marriages, in a sense: his and hers. Marriage brings improvements in men's mental health and career progress, while wives are more phobic and depressed than single women. Across classes, married women suffer more nervous breakdowns and report more nervousness, insomnia and headaches than single women.[16]

Feminist writer Rochelle Gatlin refers to women's lowered expectations as a kind of "psychological diminishment".[17] The diminishment of women's personalities in relationships has been a recurring literary theme among many women writers. Anaïs Nin, a writer intensely interested in the psychology of women, epitomised married women's psychological malaise in her work *This Hunger*. Nin was not interested in the obvious suffering of physical hunger or poverty, where personal struggles were direct and concrete. Instead she sought to portray the inner drama of "a world of diffused vision, broken connections, symbolic dramas in which the psychic vision creates totally different and elusive problems". Nin thought the basic theme of modern literature and modern life was the same: alienation – a state of "nonfeeling" dangerous to sanity and life. And so she created the character Lillian, who "felt the unreality to her of her marriage, home, and children".[18]

Adrienne Rich writes of "that female fatigue of suppressed anger and the loss of contact with her own being... partly from the discontinuity of female life with its attention to small chores, errands, work that others constantly undo, small children's constant needs."[19] Playwright and poet Sylvia Plath emphasised the kind of "mad" lucidity which can follow the loss of the romantic illusion of marriage. The character of Esther Greenwood in *The Bell Jar* states, madly and plainly, that "in spite of all the roses and kisses and restaurant dinners a man showered on a woman before he married her, what he secretly wanted when the wedding service ended was for her to flatten out underneath his feet."[20]

Through Esther, Plath sharply played upon the incongruity of man's idealising of woman on one hand, while patronising her on the other. Nin and Rich suggest that this rift threatens to bring on a complete break between emotional and physical existence, inner and external selves. Rich emphasises that the "debilitating ambivalence" women feel in this "undramatic, undramatised suffering" often leads to serious depressions and expressions that they may "go over the edge" unless the totality of their rightful selves and needs are acknowledged.[21]

We might go crazy, if that is what it takes to have the extent of our unhappiness recognised. We might go crazy, if that is what it takes for somebody to notice that we are not coping, or if that is what it takes for us to feel cared for, when we have been taking care of everyone else.

Many more women than men exhibit and are treated for "psychiatric disease". Some symptoms of schizophrenia, in particular, are now often considered psychological tactics of adjustment and adaptation to a condition of alienation – strategies of escape from the "half life" of socially determined "normality". Thus, as feminist writer and Catholic nun Madonna Kolbenschlag has noted, clinical explanations of "madness" are being qualified more and more by existential and social considerations. "What we see in some people whom we label and treat as psychotics or schizophrenics is in reality the acting out of an experiential drama that can be as much of a breakthrough as breakdown... Clinical and institutional care have largely invalidated and mutilated this kind of experience, which is primarily an experience of the soul."[22]

I think that the word "alienation" describes the consequences of the separation of women's emotional and physical being, though it is a word which many feminists have tried to avoid because of its fatalistic connotations. There is a kind of death that occurs, a separation from feeling which does not go away simply because we refuse to name it. At the centre of this numbing is our conditioning not to merge, but to submerge our own needs and feelings in order to feel for others first and foremost.

If we are honest with ourselves about some of our worst moments, we have actually had thoughts of abdicating our roles, the tasks, the drone of daily life by loosening our grip, just enough so that it all might begin to tumble, just enough so that someone has to notice our needs. I believe that there are points at which we might still have opportunities for circumstances to be addressed and needs to be recognised in a way that is less traumatic. There are windows. There are chances to address the causes of our malaise. But before we can emerge from the labyrinth of romantic relationships, I must first take you in – to a place where love and romance, hope and illusion, self and other seem indistinguishable at times.

Into the Labyrinth

❧

O NE MORNING IN 1993 the host of one of Ireland's chat-show radio programmes read a letter from a desperately lonely woman who called herself Nicki. The letter detailed Nicki's exasperation and depression over her marriage. She said she was at the end of her rope – she wanted to talk to someone, but felt unable to speak the things she thought about. Instead she wrote of her sense of emptiness and loneliness, and her desperate need to make contact with someone. Nicki asked listeners to understand that she loved her husband – a nice guy, a good man, a dutiful provider. She would never want to hurt this man, but through common neglect and disregard, their relationship had degenerated and had begun to feel empty and meaningless. Their love had become fraternal. She cared about him. She was concerned about him. But he left her feeling a terrible loneliness.

I began to hear the story of my own life being read from this other woman's letter, written by another woman's hand. She was becoming increasingly and dangerously drawn to another man, she said. What started out as daydream and fantasy was becoming a larger hope of escape and rescue. He had become the man she felt she should have been with all along. He was the man she deserved and the man who needed her. She imagined they would live a big life together, not this shrunken one. She was sure this other man felt for her as she felt for him. Over time, glances across rooms and pubs and tables had made it clear that he was equally attracted to her. In passing each other at one point, a confession had been made and he had made it clear that Nicki's interest was welcomed and reciprocated.

Now she found it impossible to carry on the lie of her marriage, yet she felt destroyed by guilt and remorse for what the relationship between herself and her husband had once been. That is what she mourned. She felt unable to carry on with the facade, but also unable to stop grieving at what had been lost. She saw herself on the threshold of desperate and exciting acts, but had paused long enough to acknowledge the sadness of her situation and to wonder if it had to be like this. Nicki asked for the advice no one could really give her, specific advice on whether or not she should stay with her husband. It might have been an easy question to answer if she had been more obviously mistreated, but the letter spoke of what sounded like real love neglected and a relationship not maintained. It seemed that they had once loved deeply.

The first two listeners' responses came from men. Both of them moralised and cautioned that this woman should remember that she was "unavailable", a married woman. There was no mention of the status of the "other man". There was no suggestion in the letter that he was any more "available" than Nicki, yet all these men could focus on was that Nicki was "confused" about her own status. Perhaps Nicki was confused, but not in the ways the callers suggested. Nicki had not temporarily forgotten her husband and marriage. She was neither mindless nor reckless, but had felt and endured the recklessness of neglect for years. She was painfully aware of the contradictions of her predicament. It was probably the very fact that she could remember what a full relationship felt like that now brought her remorse and caused her to pause at all. She hardly needed to be reminded that she was married, but she had come to know – all too well – that you are as available as you feel. This is not a matter of external dictates and is not for moralists to decide.

The essential question this woman was really asking was: does my marriage have to be like this? That was the point from which her desperation sprang. If she could find an answer to that question, she would know whether to invest herself in her marriage or a new relationship. Without an answer to that question, she might invest herself in either or both – or any other number of relationships – only to end up feeling the same emptiness. Certainly Nicki's predicament was not new to me. As the letter was read, it shook me. And I was moved when Nicki added that she was feeling terribly alone and torn, desperate for whatever help or advice listeners could offer. I wanted to reach out to Nicki and help her through her depression, make her realise that her depression was reasonable and rational. We are not crazy here. The feelings we have are not scandalous. I began to dial.

Gerry Ryan. Peg, good morning to you. How are you?

Peg Grymes. I'm a bit nervous. I was in a similar type of situation... There were problems in our relationship. I don't think there was anything that couldn't have been worked out, if we had concentrated on it. Instead what happened was that I became attracted to someone else.

G.R. Do you think you became attracted to someone else because you were put in a distracted position because of the problems, or would it have happened anyway?

P.G. To be honest, there were probably pretty severe problems in the marriage.

G.R. And this was a release of sorts?

P.G. I think it's the old story: women have affairs for romantic reasons — that is, for companionship, to feel important, to feel interesting — the more emotional reasons, perhaps.

G.R. So that happened to you. You were attracted to another man. And what did you do about it?

P.G. Well, at this point — I'm looking back on it now, and I feel like I can say, "unfortunately" — I followed through. At the time, I wouldn't have said "unfortunately". At the time it seemed like everything that I wanted. I had completely idealised and romanticised this other man into something where he became an image in my mind which didn't have much to do with the reality.

G.R. An image that was all the opposites of the current man in your life?

P.G. Well, an image that was an ideal in my head — didn't necessarily have anything to do with my husband; didn't necessarily have anything to do with the other man, in reality, either.

G.R. I think that's good of you to explain that because I think quite often men get blamed for being an image, whereas they didn't make the image, the image was made by the person who viewed them as that image.

P.G. Yes, I do think women tend to be romantics. We tend to idealise men. We tend to see ourselves in relation to our status with men. We tend to define our own selves in relation to our relationships with men. And it is not our own faults.

G.R. No?

P.G. I think we are socialised this way. But it sets you up for an awful lot of falls.

G.R. So there you were, setting yourself up for another fall.

P.G. Yes. And I know that I am not the only woman who has been in this situation.

G.R. I am sure you are not. And how did you come back from the edge?

P.G. I think, to be honest, I had to isolate myself from everyone for a little while and work on my own self. I think the problem that we sometimes have, as women, is that when there is something we need to find in our own selves, we actually think that the solution is going to be in a man – either the man we are with, or some man we could be with, some man we imagine ourselves with. When, in fact, I think the better solution is to look within ourselves. Try to develop ourselves. See what is unfulfilled within our own selves. What is it we really want to do? Could we find something that we are really good at, where we can express ourselves and do something constructive or creative?

G.R. I think you're right.

P.G. Whether or not any of our relationships survive might

be separate issues, but we do need to separate them. They have been presented to us as the same – self and man; self and marriage, children, household. So I would urge Nicki to step back from the whole situation for a while and try to cool off, because I know that when I was in the position she is in right now, I would have risked everything and given everything up to run off with this other man.

G.R. How did you step back? You thought this other guy was the solution to all your problems. What stopped you from disappearing over the sunset with him?

P.G. Well, in fact, I think he would not have disappeared over the sunset with me. I think he had entirely something else in mind. He probably had a fling or maybe a physical relation-ship in mind. He didn't have this romanticised notion of another life that I had in my head. Again, I think this leads back to the whole notion that men and women go into affairs, possibly, for different sets of reasons. Perhaps it was only me who wanted the idealised life of another existence with this man... Another problem is that you only see this person in high moments, which helps you to romanticise the whole idea of the relationship. It's very dangerous.

G.R. Did your husband discover what was happening?

P.G. Yes, he did. There were tell-tale signs. First of all, our marriage was not on the best basis at the time. There was a kind of distance. I felt kind of lonely in the marriage, in essence. What I wanted was somebody to make me feel inter-esting, to make me feel a centre of attention... even just for conversation and such. I think there is a kind of unspoken understanding of what marriage entails and that maybe it doesn't help to foster a healthy relationship. I think that, emotionally, women are left on their own a lot, maybe left with the kids. I don't mean to suggest that is worse, but sometimes it feels worse. So it leads to a kind of loneliness. Women begin to feel isolated, I think, in their relationships, in their marriages. I mean, it's bad when you feel lonely in a marriage.

G.R. You were lonely.

P.G. Yes, I think I wanted to feel important and interesting.

G.R. You couldn't draw this from your husband?

P.G. I tried. I think I tried to get that idea through to him.

G.R. But it's not an easy thing to respond to. Because a lot of the time a man will say, "What's wrong?" or "What are you talking about?" and it's not that he's being careless or that he is stupid. It's that he genuinely doesn't know what you are talking about.

P.G. Maybe he doesn't even sense that there is, particularly, a problem. Maybe the marriage, as it exists, does fulfil his expectations of what marriage was going to be. The affair that I had really functioned to set off all the bells and buzzers – stemming from the imbalance of it all – that we were at the brink of losing it. But still there was so much holding us together. Though I don't think it should have had to, perhaps it did take the possibility of losing it all to make us realise the worth of our relationship. If he would meet me half-way, then we still had a possibility. I think it took a big jolt to realise that.[1]

I was not calling myself a feminist when I rang that radio programme. I was not calling myself a feminist when I heard the story of my greatest crisis echoed in the words of another woman's letter. Perhaps I had been too enmeshed in the details of my own life to see any larger pattern or recognise that pattern in other women's lives. But the voice I heard coming from me and being broadcast on the radio was unmistakable and clear, informed by thousands of women over decades of their own specific experiences.

In *Outrageous Acts and Everyday Rebellions*, Gloria Steinem predicted the importance of such jolts and other politicising events in the lives of young women – events through which she believes women will confront the feminism within themselves.[2] Call it what you will – intuition, an innate sense of fairness, justice, vision – it is the strength which women will draw upon to survive and change circumstances which become unbearable. These women might not be calling themselves "feminists", but their standard of what is acceptable will have been shaped and influenced by the women's movement and a long tradition of feminist thought.

Why had I not recognised myself, drawing upon the resources willed to me by consciously acting and thinking women? Perhaps until the information these feminists left for me seemed immediately relevant, even vital, I could not grasp it fully. Indeed, we might find our feminist strength when we are at our lowest, when we have exhausted the resources we are accustomed to drawing upon, and need to find new ways to survive.

The reason for the "unreality" of our existence is obscured in a socialisation which is traditional and seems "normal". And while some of us remain unable to name our malady and others refuse to do so, the rhetoric of feminism has become something which, very often, seems either irrelevant to many women or ridiculous in its own contradictions.

Recently women who call themselves feminists have become feminism's greatest critics. It used to be that only chauvinists would suggest that feminists were women who hated men; now there are feminists who say as much. There are feminists who blame other feminists for taking the excitement and interest out of sex. These "neo-conservative" feminists believe – and have tried to convince the rest of us – that we have embraced "victim" status, incorporated victimhood into the feminist self-image, exaggerated women's oppression, and derived some kind of status from all of this. There is a danger that such perspectives may produce a spectacular backlash against feminism in many countries, including those that have not had much of a "lash" to begin with.

Over the last decade, even when we have not had to combat ideological reactions against feminism, there seems to be an absence of feminist consciousness and a reluctance amongst young women to identify as feminists. Holland and Eisenhart's study suggests that it is not easy for people to recognise other women or men who share their reservations about gender relations. They found that "Terms did exist that indicated a stance toward the women's movement, like 'libber' and 'feminist', but even these terms tended to be absorbed into the [romantic] model as indicating types of women who were not very sexy." They add that "there was little talk of the women's movement" and that the lack of interest which they noted was "typical for campuses at the time... [F]eminist activity, although present, was the work of a small minority of faculty and students."[3]

Women tended to turn to other women, Holland and Eisenhart found, mainly as a support group for orchestrating the "main activities – activities with men". Once a woman "fell in love" or found a boyfriend, she became embroiled in the ups and downs of the relationship itself and often enlisted the support of girlfriends at that point. Yet even that degree of sisterhood was difficult for many women to maintain as they struggled to keep control of their own personal affairs; they hesitated to trust and share experiences with other women.

But there were exceptions. Kandace was cynical about romance and explained why friendships, particularly with women, were important to her: "[F]riendships were important for acknowledging my existence... showing me that I had a purpose because I had an effect on their lives, and they had an effect on mine... They were important in helping me to find out who 'me' is."[4] Another woman, Sandy, was disillusioned about the way romantic relationships often worked out. When relationships went sour, she said she tried to "pour strength" into her girlfriends to make them feel secure.[5]

These moments in feminism beg us to take a closer look at the development of feminism today – including the counter-revolutionary impulse – not only in order to understand women's disaffection from progressive feminism but also to consider and grasp the opportunities that exist for a third wave. The best way I know to consider the development of feminism is in a way that is personal, by tracing the development of my own feminism, all of which sprang from moments of identification with other women's predicaments.

Consider the radio programme's next caller on that November morning: she called from the bare floor which she had chosen to sleep upon. She could no longer lie with her husband. She described the love she felt for him and told us that she had never wanted to hurt him or offend their marriage, but was afraid that she easily could. She spoke of feeling that same sense of loneliness in marriage that I had described. She said that she was empty, exhausted and unable to carry on. She had imagined escaping. She could also imagine her weakness at the possibility of romance, and so she was taking herself away for a while. This caller dreaded the kind of confusion Nicki and I had related and hoped that time away from her husband would help her decide what mattered. She just wanted to be alone with her own thoughts for a while. But even in this last effort, she felt a kind of guilt, as though she was choosing between what she needed for her own life and what others had come to expect.

This was a woman trying to make a journey back into her original thoughts and intentions, rather than shrivel under the constant pressure of disillusion. She was not trying to escape, but was taking the considered actions necessary to gain control and take responsibility for her own future. I thought this caller was fortunate. She still had the opportunity to turn to her self instead of grasping at further illusions. And how sensible she seemed – to know that she needed to be alone with herself, even in the midst of her grief. I wished I could be back at that "before" stage with her, to determine my own path again.

In fact there were many times when I just wanted to go back to some more simple, less complicated time in my life. Often I would think back on my childhood and imagine myself as an innocent again. I was born in New York, the seventh and youngest child in an Irish-American home. My father was a cop in New York City. He liked working nights because day and evening shifts were "boring". My mother was a secretary, so it was my father who was home with me during the day when I was a toddler. I watched cartoons while he tried to sleep sometimes and straightened the house other times. He liked things tidy. He was a good man, essentially.

Don't get me wrong. My father was not a saint or anything. He was never a perfect man. Like his own father and mother, he drank too much. We didn't call it alcoholism, it was just the way he was. When he drank, he was the sort of man who became a bit too full of thoughts. I remember sitting in his big armchair with him. I may have been seven or eight years old. He started to get up and I helped him to the kitchen. He stumbled a bit and sat down on a step – began telling me that he was "not a young man" and wouldn't "be around much longer". I ran upstairs, crying, and told my mother that Daddy was talking about silly, scary things. She told me he was just tired and then she tucked me into bed.

My father died the following year at the age of fifty-two. He had been raking up the leaves in our yard on an ordinary day in March when he fell over with a heart attack and never got up. I remember that day very well; it was just coming up to St Patrick's Day, 1973. My father collected my sister and me from school as usual. On the way home my father had to stop at the dry cleaner to get a special suit which he was having pressed for a St Patrick's Day dance. I remember the suit, too, because it was very unusual and really awful. I still can't imagine my father wearing that green velour jacket and matching bow-tie – only for the sake of St Patrick's Day, I guess. After finishing at the dry cleaner, my father went into the local bakery and got my sister and me a couple of large cookies – half vanilla-frosted and half chocolate-frosted. The cookies were very sweet, with that thick, hard frosting – the sort of thing you can't stomach much past the age of ten or so. I was still only nine, so it seemed tasty to me. My sister was thirteen and had started watching her weight. She didn't want hers, so I got to have two.

It was the same after-school schedule for me every day – *Flintstones, Gilligan's Island, Beverly Hillbillies*, right up until dinner-time. This day I took a break to thank my dad for the cookies. But when I looked out into the backyard, I could see my father already on the ground, the rake having fallen at his side. I ran to get my sister: she didn't like me to come near her bedroom, but I knew this time it was important. I remember approaching the closed door, knocking hurriedly and shouting that something was wrong with Daddy. My sister told me to run to the neighbours' house for help. I knew then that it was going to be awful. I remember running through the leaves, legs like lead, begging God not to let my father die. I watched his body jump when the paramedics placed the electric paddles on his chest and I knew then that he was dead. I knew there was no way that my dad's body would ever just jolt like that, with no real response from him. If he was okay, he would have jumped up and decked somebody, I figured. But he didn't. He died in the yard, beside the slate patio he had built. It's probably typical. Lots of husbands and fathers probably die there, in their yards, beside the patios they build. And it's then that the women around them must find new resources of their own.

My mother was left with five daughters still dependent on her and her salary as a secretary. Somehow she managed to cope with things well enough so that by the time I reached my teens, she was able to afford the fees for university. I went to the University of California at Berkeley, with my mother supporting me all the way through my undergraduate education. My mother paid her money and expected good results. The results were good, but perhaps not exactly what she expected. By the time I graduated, Berkeley had turned out yet another "long-haired thinker" – another radical lefty who didn't seem to have much in common any longer with her mother, her family, or her government. When I called myself a socialist, my mother interpreted "communist" and that meant "un-American". If my mother could have demanded her money back from the University of California, she might have done so.

After having finished my undergraduate degree at Berkeley in 1985, I took the obligatory European back-packing vacation with a girlfriend from home. I came to Ireland the same way most Americans do: as a tourist. And I met the man I would eventually marry in the way a lot of people do – when I was on vacation in a place I didn't know well. Maybe I was a bit more relaxed than usual. Maybe my defenses were down. He was a local and he was helpful to me. Still, I wasn't really looking for anyone when I first met Liam.

At the time, Liam seemed to be everything anyone would have hoped for in a companion. He was literate, intelligent, sensitive, handsome. He combined many of the qualities that I would have imagined in a husband, if I had imagined one. I resisted that tendency. I had become used to the idea of being alone. I was extremely studious. Because I rarely dated and felt I was not popular with men, I figured that I should not anticipate male companionship in my life. I was terribly lonely but convinced myself that I had no interest in any man if a relationship would dull my own sense of ambition. I guess I was like those women in Holland and Eisenhart's study, postponing my involvement in the romantic world because the entire scheme made me feel a bit uncomfortable.

So when Liam first came into my life, I pretended not to notice much. I literally bumped into him in the street. He thought I needed some help, so he carried my bags. He asked me to meet him that evening and I agreed, but I didn't show up. The next day, he sought me out and again helped me carry my bags. Over the next few days we became friends and gradually began to feel more than friends.

Liam grew up in the midst of the "troubles" in a nationalist area of Northern Ireland. He told me stories of crawling to school with a handkerchief over his nose and mouth to dodge the tear gas. I had come from a very different environment, one of relative comfort. Whether I felt empathy or some kind of guilt I am not sure, but it did seem natural enough to want to embrace that little boy and look after him. How could you not?

As we got to know more about each other, I could not help but notice that he was "fond of the drink". That's how it's put, sounds nice and friendly, sociable and all. In this, he was just like so many of the people around him and like so many of the people around me. Even that seemed natural – familiar, at least. My own family had been plagued by alcoholism. As the youngest in my family, I had wanted to help so many of the people I loved, but felt unable to speak or be taken seriously, and was afraid to take on matters that were too enormous for me to cope with. It seemed to be my mother's mission to try to protect me and spare me any trauma, and my responsibility to pretend that nothing was affecting me.

My mother had done her best to insulate the young ones from alcoholism, to minimise conflict and to contain the chaos that would, inevitably and despite her efforts, affect each of us in some way. Its effect on me was that when I met a man who reminded me of my family's difficulties, I needed to help him. I never even noticed that I was replicating my mother's caretaking role for myself.

I was starting to relive my mother's life – but, somehow, I didn't see things that way. Did things seem so different because now I was in a new role as the nurse and there was a new patient? Or did I not care to notice? Perhaps the relationship served purposes I could not face. Perhaps this relationship created an illusion of control for me – a kind of negative free-dom. In this relationship I could hold the moral high ground, criticising Liam's drinking and, at the same time, maintain the strange illusion of control that I felt when the pattern was fulfilled. I could get angry and demand changes, knowing that the "changes" were really only temporary adjustments to what Liam viewed as my "moods". There would be some talk of turning "new leaves", though a short period of good behav-iour is all there ever really was. Knowing the "good behav-iour" would not last, I went on feeling superior for living my model life – keeping everything running smoothly and "normally" in the household, just as my mother had. And so on. And so on. These days they'd call me the "co-dependent".

I am not the first and will not be the last to replicate the patterns of dysfunction. Just as the fetishist follows a beautiful foot, scarcely noticing the whole woman, each of us may respond to some trait in a man – all of it spinning out from our first need, directing us, enslaving us, until we choose to unravel such webs and free ourselves. There are ways to unravel the traumas that have crystallised in damaging patterns, but until you dig up and confront your obsessions, you cannot become conscious of old, unchosen patterns and begin to leave them behind. It will not be easy, as Steinem cautions: "Old patterns, no matter how negative and painful they may be, have an incredible magnetic power – because they do feel like home."[6]

Okay, maybe Liam was and maybe he wasn't exactly "Mr Right". But, just as Holland and Eisenhart might have predicted for me, I had met a young man whom I didn't mind spending time with and vice versa. He was handsome. I was attracted to him; he was attracted to me. If there were devils, they were devils I knew – warm, cuddly, familiar devils. Besides, most of us have to take the leap some time, and at least this guy solved some problems for me. No longer did I have to be "on the scene", "on the block" or – worst of all – "on the shelf". Even when I went back to university, I could take the promise of this relationship with me. We wrote to each other every week and phoned often. In this way my first serious dalliance – my first dangerous venture into this uncomfortable world of romance – was also my retreat. There I was, the magnificent exception, beginning to take on patterns which were not supposed to be about me. And as this relationship became more and more serious, both Liam and I seemed to want it that way.

Imagining that "love" would fix everything, I made the fairly common mistake of marrying a man I wanted to help. I fell into the trap of believing I could change someone in order to prove something about myself – and believing that if he did change, everything that was ever wrong would finally be resolved. I dashed my head against this hope for years. Meanwhile, I was not centred on my own life and what I might do with it, but on controlling his life and resolving his problems. This is common to women who "marry their lives instead of leading them".[7]

I was not alone in finding something familiar in this relationship. Liam had been raised in the midst of political events that reached in from the streets to his family's kitchen. While his mother was a dominant figure at home, she was also active in the Irish Civil Rights Movement of the late 1960s and '70s. Sometimes her sons and daughter had to wait their turns while she carried on with a struggle that she saw as urgent and intimately linked to the work of raising a family of Irish children and citizens. It was not a family's fault that the outside world was so critically distorted as to require so much of a mother's attention, but Liam was left needing more of the attention of a woman like her – smart, outwardly strong, ambitious. I suppose that in those ways and in other ways that I still do not fully understand, I fit the bill.

For better or worse, we "clicked" in ways that were determined before we met and had as much to do with other people as ourselves. We had those kinds of complementary needs that are bound to make a relationship of some sort. Each of our pasts had established a set of characters and cues which mixed with romantic culture and could be conveniently discussed in terms of "love". Perhaps it is this complex, emotive symbolism from our pasts that explains the ghostliness and abstraction of some of our present relationships. At times many of us have felt that we are not living with real, whole human beings. We feel that someone is there, but not really there, not really engaged at all.

Perhaps what worried me about my relationship with Liam – more than all the other abstractions and aspects of mutual neediness – was the fact that I loved him because he was happy. Whatever happened to him and however difficult his life had been, he was happy. He was happier than I thought I would ever be. Liam's chin was higher and his attitude lighter than I could ever imagine mine. He was able to go out and take a bite of life and simply enjoy, while I really needed to be reminded of the lightness of life. I hoped that by being around Liam, some of his lightness might rub off on me. At the same time, Liam loved me because, with me, he felt comfortable enough to admit that much of the lightness was an act, a protection and denial of the incomprehensible weight of some of his own thoughts. He was falsely happy, and I was distortedly sad.

When Liam and I decided to marry, I convinced myself that I was not compromising my other aspirations but was integrating him into my life. He really did become a part of my self, more than I expected. We spent the early years of our marriage in Ireland, and I spent my nights and weekends forming our household, attending to the details of our lives together. I put my time, energy and money into making each of the homes we lived in a place that Liam would want to come home to at the end of each day. Despite my best efforts, Liam still preferred the pub as much as he had before we moved in together and married. Each evening, I was left to feel more unattractive and worse company than the night before. But I still imagined that the proper home and the proper wife would coax him home. Then I set about becoming that wife – making myself into an image which I imagined would satisfy Liam's need for woman's love.

What I had not anticipated were the ways in which Liam's combined need for drink and women's attentions would kill my confidence and drive me to the edge of my self. I never imagined that my love and attention would not be enough for a man. I suppose that I had believed I would be a man's answer – the resolution of his needs for approval and acceptance. But Liam's needs just went right on past me. When Liam did seem "taken" by a woman, and played upon her attentions, I would watch and study her as my new objective. I would go home and try to form myself, "improve" myself, change myself into the woman Liam seemed to desire. Even when I found him looking straight into the eyes of another woman, I was angry and hurt, but instead of pouring drinks over heads or walking out, I studied from a distance.

I was a good student, as usual. If the new attraction was blonde, give me a few days and I would be blonde too. If she was dark, I would be dark over the weekend. If she was thin, I would try to lose weight. I would study the way she put herself together and try to dress as she did, or wear jewellery as I never had before. All the while, the contortions I performed and disguises I fashioned brought me no comfort in my own beauty. Without some core of self-esteem, I felt sure that it was only a matter of time before Liam would leave for someone prettier, younger, less heavy in thought, or otherwise "better" than me. Because I could never form an image that suited me and satisfied Liam, I blamed myself for not being the wife he needed. For as long as his desires seemed to be my shortcomings, I suffered needlessly from his promiscuities. I never looked critically enough at the fact that, as much as I tried to be everywoman, I could never satisfy what was actually an insatiable neediness.

I have seen men and women alike place their hopes in romantic love and then set about living out a kind of Don Juanism. One love is not enough, two are not enough, neither are three, and all in response to insecurities and needs that distance us from our abilities to form true relationships. Inevitably, there is no love big enough, deep enough, strong enough.

"So much of our lives is spent in a longing and a search – for what, we do not know. So many of our ostensible 'goals', so many of the things we want, turn out to be the masks behind which our real desires hide; they are symbols for the actual values and qualities for which we hunger. They are not reducible to physical or material things, not even to a physical person; they are psychological qualities: love, truth, honesty, loyalty, purpose – something we can feel is noble, precious, and worthy of our devotion. We try to reduce all this to something physical – a house, a car, a better job, or a human being, but it doesn't work."[8]

I did not realise, then, that Liam's needs would never be fulfilled, as the vacuum inside of him would never be filled without understanding its causes. All the while, as a woman, I blamed myself for not being able to apply my own emotional and intellectual skills to making our marriage "work".

Over months and years, the mere details of our household became the only aspects of our relationship that seemed particularly real. I took great care of our home. Sometimes it seemed to be all the evidence I had to prove our shared existence. I examined every atom of our home life with the kind of anxious, analytic zeal that no love can endure. Petty matters took on gigantic proportions. One day I asked Liam where he thought I should hang a new photograph. Here? There? He had no preference. I insisted that these are the things people should care about: "It should matter to you. These four walls are your home. How can you not have an opinion?" None of it had the significance for him that it had for me. Friends would try to explain that men just don't care about such matters and don't notice details, but that was not an answer for me. I kept trying to prove a point.

When our son was born, I thought no one would be able to deny the significance of this addition to our home. A big part of me hoped that a child would cement the basic love that must have been in our relationship, somewhere. Like so many women, I thought a child would give us more in common and lend meaning to our union. That might be true of a marriage that is good to begin with, but bring a child into a relationship that is already on the rocks and you find more to argue about, a heightening of your emotions, and an even greater disappointment and accentuated feeling of abandonment when things continue to go badly.

Now two of us were left alone at home. Sometimes my son and I were sufficient companionship for each other. Other times, my resentment grew as I saw myself – intelligent, ambitious, attractive – left to my "double duty" of work and domesticity while my husband seemed to be the one with time to have a life of his own. Sometimes I thought that education and intelligence should have delivered me from this fate. Other times it seemed all the more reason why the weight of "making this work" was on me. I argued with myself that I should have known better – and if I could not have known better, I should at least be able to think my way through all of this.

I thought I might reason with, cajole or force Liam to be a different and more equitable kind of husband. He claimed to be a "new man" so I decided I would make him live up to his political correctness. If he would not take part in our family and domestic life, I would become just as unemotional and then coldly, determinedly, insist that he deliver me some equality. I wanted a life, too. The problem was that I did not know how to articulate the need for "a life" beyond my routine of work inside and outside our home. It always had seemed to boil down to "nights out" for Liam, so I insisted on my own nights out, even though I have never enjoyed going out as much as I enjoy a bit of peace and quiet, cuddling up with a book, a bit of music in the background.

After many tears, hugs and regretful admissions that he had not "realised" my unhappiness, Liam happily granted my modest request. Nights out I wanted, nights out I got. And so I set out on activities that I have never really enjoyed and have never found relaxing. I prettied and preened myself and was off. As lonely as ever, I forced myself into a pub, muttering: "You have come out to enjoy yourself and you will enjoy yourself."

The Cult of Man's Love

❧

IN 1932, IN the midst of a torrid love affair with Henry
Miller, Anaïs Nin wrote in her journal: "When he got
hungry, I offered to cook the dinner. 'Let me play at being
the wife of a genius.' And I went to the kitchen in my stately
rose dress."[1]

Romanticising our relationships with men to the extent that
they seem to be the very meaning of life itself, is the malady
which makes our lives a drama of diminished expectations.
Often, it is only in moments of complete disillusion that
romance is revealed as the major source of women's helplessness and dependencies. In this entire romantic exercise, it is
hard to understand how we have ever seen anything heroic,
honourable or quaint.

As I have tried to become more aware of my own self, the
authentic needs of my self, the things that I like in people and

the things that exhaust me, I feel stronger and better able to resist the melodrama and illusion of romance. I could vow that I will never again engage in relationships that require my self to be submerged, but doing so denies the nature of consciousness as a process. To be conscious of your self is not something you do in one day, and then everything falls neatly into place, all your problems solved. It is something that requires constant effort and awareness. Consciousness is something intentional; it demands focus. It is a human possibility, but not a certainty.

Romance only stops gaps and distracts us from the deeper search into self. So many of us alchemise into romantic projections exactly those qualities which we ourselves require: faith, hope, ambition, interest. In this way, romance keeps us both from looking deeper within ourselves and looking more critically at a society that has fostered the vicarious existence of women in a masculine world. In short, romance makes us passive; it replaces action in self-realisation and work toward self-determination.

I've never been immune. Having forced myself into a pub one day, and drunk a little gin, eventually I gave myself permission to phone for a taxi to take me home. Just then I recognised some of Liam's friends at a table and nodded to them. When I finished my call and turned to leave the bar, one of the men said loudly enough for me to hear: "Why, she's a happily married woman..." I turned my head, wondering if they could be talking about me. He spoke again. "Peggy, this man here thinks you're lovely looking." I walked out of that bar not sure who had made the comment, and not wanting to be too dangerously aware of any man who thought I was lovely. It was enough to know that someone did. I was cured, healed for the moment, walking on air.

I was doing our grocery shopping a week later, after a day at work, when one of the men who had been in the pub approached me. He looked into my eyes, stopped and stood in one spot as though his feet had suddenly become cemented to the pavement. "Peg..." was all he said. I wanted to, but couldn't, turn my eyes away from his. My knees felt weak and I had a tremendous impulse to concentrate, somehow, and get on with my errands. I wanted to tell him, "All right, all right, I know what is happening here. Now leave me alone. It's too much." Instead I walked away without saying anything.

But I couldn't get that man out of my mind. I thought about him, too much. He became the romance that filled my life, though I rarely saw him. Passing him in the street became the random occurrence that I looked forward to. Each day that I went into town, I prepared excitedly for the unlikely possibility that we might see each other at a distance.

My torn and treacherous feelings became more than I could cope with. I knew I should be concentrating on my marriage. I decided to convince Liam that we should leave Ireland and try life in the US for a while. I was convinced that this was the solution to a range of problems: it would take me away from the confusing attraction I felt for this other man, and at the same time take Liam out of the Irish pub culture and away from the companions he lived with more than me.

I should have known that to get away from pub culture you would have to go a lot further than New York City. Liam became homesick and only drank more, to later hours than the Irish pubs had allowed. Then he walked home through streets that were more dangerous than the ones we had left in Ireland. We had changed venue, but the problems at the core of our relationship were the same as ever. I became even more unhappy as I was forced to realise that the problems we had were inherent. We could not solve them by changing jobs, or houses, or even countries. Now I felt really stuck. We argued more often, more loudly and with more resentment; there was less and less holding us together. I resorted to nagging a lot of the time, all the while blaming Liam for turning me into "the kind of woman" who does nothing but complain. Liam felt hen-pecked, pressured, disliked. I continued to let everything hinge on the idea that he might change and that then our real life together might begin, but I had less and less hope now.

Not long after moving to New York, I met a man who found me interesting and knew how to make his interest clear. He was an artist – a painter and illustrator. I first met him at a John Martyn concert at a club in downtown Manhattan. It is funny and strange to remember that, at first, I found him annoying as he stared at me so intently and incessantly from the bar. I was so annoyed with all of men's flirtations I thought about plucking his eyes out. When I went up to order a drink, the fellow with the stare insisted on paying. I went over to him then and asked if he had something to say to me. He said he had: that he had never seen me before and might not ever see me again, unless he took a chance of making sure that we did. He said he thought I was beautiful and that he dreamed of and imagined a woman who looked like me. He was very polite, but also quite forward and, at that point, that was what I wanted.

His name was Evan. We may have invented some innocent

pretence for the next meeting we arranged. I can't really remember it, if there was one. Anyone would have seen through it anyway. For me, it was a night out. On that evening, as he ran his finger down my back, I froze and melted at the same time. It had been so long since I felt such good company. I suppose I was also desperate to feel some kind of "love", though I knew I should keep it within limits, in some kind of control. For the moment, I did not worry. I felt lovely, no matter what.

For a while I still felt lovely enough that nothing could get me down, not even Liam. We argued less often and, in many ways, our relationship seemed better. There was less stress and anger in the air. I was happier than I had been for a long time. I felt my own value and worth. It was as though I had been given a second opinion and been found interesting and good company after all. In many ways, a bit of romance was tremendous therapy, of a temporary sort.

Still the pressures and difficulties of life and work in New York started to overwhelm our little family unit. We worked harder than ever, but saved nothing; both of us wanted to quit our jobs. The expense of child-care and housing, and the continued decline of our marriage, led us to decide to return to Ireland where we still owned a house. Liam and I agreed then that we would not live together in Ireland; that a separation might help us decide what mattered in our relationship and whether or not we could fix it. Liam went back to Ireland first, saying he would get a flat and start working on himself. Later I returned to the house we owned there. Our son? We made the only decision we could – to share him, as best we could. This, we imagined, was a way to minimise the disruption for him, until we decided what we wanted to do with the shreds of our lives.

Liam and I argued because we felt tremendous stress between still loving each other on many levels, but losing faith in our relationship. We argued over petty things and larger things. Why did I have to hear of his women friends and the parties he went to? During his time with our son, was he leaving our son with his grandparents while carrying on with his own plans? These and other similar points filled our exchanges. It really did not matter what we argued about. The essence of it all was that I had become too cynical to believe that Liam would ever be sober, or satisfied with the affection and love of one woman.

Often I blamed myself for Liam's troubles. It seemed that he no longer even had the capacity for the simple happiness that I had envied and been so strongly attracted to. I often felt I would never forgive myself for making him sad. With me, I believed he had bitten off more than he could chew. I had concluded that I was probably a difficult and tortured person to live with. I imagined that almost anyone else might have simpler needs, make fewer demands, would suit him better. I thought some sort of simple marriage to a "simple" woman might have been bliss for him – no complaints, no expectations. I began to give up on our relationship and lovingly, I thought, let him go.

We both believed that once a marriage is broken, there is no fixing it. We believed there is no repairing or compensating for grave offenses. And we had both offended each other so deeply and for so long, we could hardly remember any of the reasons we had had for loving each other. The fact that we did still feel a kind of love for each other seemed to make everything much worse and more confusing. It seemed impossible to stay together, and impossible to part. I pointed out other women to Liam, partly to punish myself for my own infidelity, but also in the hope that some "simple woman" might come into his life – finally and permanently – and make our decision for us.

Yet, as much as I hoped for a "simple woman", I did not find her anywhere. Perhaps some of us are more likely to "complain" than others; perhaps some know better than others that we have a right to our expectations; but no one I ever noticed seemed "simple". Pretty soon I realised that I had to stop trying to make distinctions between myself and other kinds of women. This was the beginning of a feminism I had neither sought nor imagined I would have cared to find.

As women, we are acutely aware of the tyranny of appearances; no one could be better placed than ourselves to put forward a challenge for communication beyond this level. Now I recognise the degree to which pleasures I remember most strongly with Evan were moments of satisfied vanity, while anxieties sprang from personal jealousies, and my mood flung maniacally between the two. All of this only dawned on me in a confusion that brought the reality of the beauty myth home to me.

While I lived apart from Liam, I still had contact with Evan by telephone and letters. One evening Evan and I were talking over antiquated telephone lines after a long period without any contact at all. Excitedly, we both began to speak at the same time. I imagined that he was feeling as I was, seeking unlikely declarations and impossible reassurances. The echo over the telephone lines made it difficult to understand each other, so he had to repeat: "Do you still keep your hair long?" What a disappointment I felt in being asked a question which had nothing to do with me – not really *me*.

It was a while longer before I really began to question my judgement of Evan, and that only after I began to question his mental stability. He would call me at two or three o'clock in the morning, always high on pot. I took this as confirmation that he thought of me when he was really needy and vulnerable. I was so fawning that I would speak to him whenever he called. It seemed my privilege to speak to him even during these artificially-induced moments of emotion. Only later could I see that I was merely a convenience, an outlet for what he could not deal with in more conscious moments. Sometimes he would roar and cry down the telephone to me and I would consider it my special role to receive his human utterances.

But there were some things I could not romanticise, even in my wildest imagination. Evan was constantly getting into drunken arguments and fights with people who were supposed to be his friends. Before him, I had never known anyone who had been in a physical brawl. I'll admit that in that sense I may have lived a sheltered life, but I liked it just that way. I sometimes blamed incidents on the company he had been keeping, but this man always seemed to be with the wrong crowd. One night when he called me after one of his fights, I slept through the ringing of the telephone. The answering machine picked up and Evan left a curt, angry message: "Call me, now. Now! Right now." It was impossible to romanticise this one. It is true that when you know someone well, have been familiar with his dreams, you might not be removed enough to begin to recognise the signs of his madness. But this time I did sense it. It was part of my most basic upbringing and understanding that no one should speak to me in such a demanding, controlling voice. I would never have allowed my husband to talk to me in that tone. I was glad for the message that was finally beginning to get through: Evan had no respect for me.

When Gloria Steinem analysed her attraction to a very wrong man, she reasoned: "If I had been drawn to a man totally focused on his own agenda, maybe I needed to have an agenda of my own... If I had been drawn to simple-minded fun and dancing, maybe I should get off the treadmill and ask myself the revolutionary question: What do I enjoy?" Steinem's self-analysis gave her the impetus to make time to do some of the things she loved. Finally, she walked away from a romance understanding a pattern: "I do know that I chose an opposite as a dramatic example of what I missed in myself."[2]

Even after all of this, it was still a while longer before I really understood my attraction to this very wrong man. I mean, whether or not I was going to be with my husband and whether or not my marriage could have been made to work again, Evan would never have been the right person for me. And yet, the attraction felt very real and strong. This affair was not simply a matter of my wanting someone else, anyone else, a bit of company and attention. If it had been as simple as that, there were other opportunities I might have pursued. There were definite qualities that drew me to Evan, though these were not qualities unique to him; indeed, in many ways the affair de-personalised him too.

A lot of it had to do with the fact that he was an artist. My friends and I are only now beginning to understand, and not simply chuckle at, our almost pathological attraction to musicians and artists. My attraction to Evan and other painters, writers and musicians has always had everything to do with my own need for creativity and artistry in my life. Being socialised in the same ways most women are socialised, I supposed that a man would bring these and other qualities to my door.

I found a rescuing feminist moment when I read an excerpt from a lecture Nin presented at Sonoma College in California in 1973: "When I once said I would rather be married to an artist then be one, I was really being a coward. I was really dropping out. I was saying that I would help the artist but I was not going to try to be one. There was nothing wonderful or sacrificial about that... I decided I would be the helper, the assistant; it was really much easier... After a while I realised Miller wasn't going to write the book I wanted to write..."[3]

The mystique of the artist as "eccentric" made the situation all the more dangerous as it provided all kinds of allowances for Evan's outrageous mood swings and occasional callousness. I would never have been so generous and patient with myself as I was with my young artist. I feel a real grief now when I consider how I wanted creativity, but did not seek to discover my own. Instead, my greatest aspiration was to support and nurture the creativity of a man. What seemed an aesthetic experience is now an embarrassment. I have to admit this, especially now that I understand the pathology and cannot afford even to chuckle.

I feel that much more duped when I look back critically and realise that the creative genius I fixated on has produced very little of his own work. Most of the paintings he actually finished were only good copies of well-known originals. He only sang and played tunes that had always been "beat". Now I can see his imitations were not signs of creativity, but of a cynical satisfaction with semblance rather than creation. I have had to ask myself the hard questions that could lead me out of illusion: to what degree was I responsible for creating and following an image of Evan? Had I cast my own desires upon him? Did I imagine this person?

This "creative genius" was a figment of my own fervid imagination. There was an idea called Evan, which I had endowed with creative qualities and supreme sensitivity. I had begun to notice him when I was at a critical low in my self-esteem, so much eroded by the loneliness of my marriage that I felt an almost complete emptiness. Steinem notes that it is at such times that we are most prone to fall back on the romantic rescue fantasies of affairs and other relationships of imbalance and illusion.[4]

Ours was just one small example of the ways in which relationships are distorted to become some kind of quick-fix for self and image. In the larger picture, the disease of women's separate selves leads us to romantic projection and disconnection from the qualities we most want for ourselves. We have become passive in dangerous, self-deprecating ways as we cling to the notion that men will bring the qualities we desire into our lives. At the same time, men have been made to believe that they have what "their" woman possesses: youth, beauty or compassion, perhaps. These projections de-personalise all of us, press impossible demands upon our partners, and submerge vital aspects of our own selves.

No person can fulfil the life and self of another, any more than one can live the life of another. The romantic model of love, in teaching us to define ourselves in relation to men, is regressive and limiting. In the romantic model, an independent woman is a contradiction in terms; the very idea of the intrinsic worth of women as individuals is an affront. Rather, women have been encouraged to nurture and sustain loving relationships and, because we are supposed to care more than men do, we are also the first to feel guilty and inadequate when personal or familial relationships are not going well.

There is little room in this scheme for a woman to feel or express ambivalence. Ambivalence would be selfish and anti-social. Faced with this kind of social pressure, many women cannot express discontent with their roles in clear, conscious ways. Discontent simply festers in a vague, generalised depression, or diffuses into desperate, romantic rescue fantasies. Either way, gender roles are not questioned, while untold numbers of women are considered "disturbed", "mad", "irresponsible" and "deviant". As women, we are presented with an impossible situation when our relationships are accompanied by this doomed-to-failure scenario in which all self-sacrifice is good and self-interest is selfish, egocentric, narcissistic. This is the inherent imbalance of our relationships. There is no space here for growth and self-discovery.

Before I felt and discovered the roots of my own vulnerability in the imbalance of my marriage, I clung to a kind of smug and shallow confidence that I was too smart, too well-educated, too articulate to fall victim to gender roles and romantic preoccupations. Somehow I thought intelligence and degrees would carry me above all that and exempt me from the lessons of my own culture. Yet never before had I so lacked imagination as when I was faced with frustration and alienation in my marriage. And I responded to my lack of self-esteem and longings for intimacy in the predictable ways. It seemed that in order to feel good about myself, I needed a man.

Like many women before me, I feel the pain of looking back on long, vulnerable years when I valued myself according to my place in the lives of men. Passion was the solace for companionship in my life, as romance was the crystallisation of my imperfect desires. But I must not see it all as wasted time. I would never want to learn to feel less, nor even to feel less hurt, but I do know that I can learn to avoid unnecessary suffering in romance. And I also know that even the blunders I have made – the foolish, desperate, romantic, unwise actions – have led me somewhere. Every lesson I learn about myself is part of shaking off the very heavy sleep from which women must awaken in order to overcome our illusions. As women we must either grow together and within ourselves, or turn to externals. It all depends on the ways in which we do or do not work out the moral themes of our lives, not in terms of imposed moralities, but in relation to our own integrity.

Under the cover of seduction and romance, some of us pursue self-protection – to control instead of being controlled, to conquer instead of being conquered. We end up adopting the same frail foundation upon which too many men build their egos, and become like the men who believe: if I conquer this woman, or that woman, I have conquered everything; I will possess all that I want. All we are doing is substituting our feminine personae for more masculine ones, and our choices are still cast in terms of roles, our options limited by them.

Rather than questioning the tenuous bases of these choices and determining our own values, we resort to costume and decoration. But in all of our elaborate machinations we only create more roles for ourselves – further dissonances and deviations – when what we need is sincerity and naturalness.

It is helpful to consider the predicaments and pretenses of Anaïs Nin's life in relation to our own cult-like dependencies upon men, not because Nin always knew how to live, but because she began to waken from that sleep of illusion. She recognised that she was not fated to be vulnerable to romantic roles and she sought ways out of that labyrinth. She wrote that when she talked about living out all instincts, "it was all just steam". She admitted that she followed only "the most accessible thread" in romance and came no closer to her true self.

Nin reflected upon the ways that romance reduced the complexity of living: "It amazes me that when Henry walks towards the café table where I wait for him, or opens the gate to our house, the sight of him is sufficient to exult me. No letter from anyone, even in praise of my book, can stir me as much as a note from him."[5] Certainly it suited Henry Miller that Nin wished only to serve him as his wife. When he fantasised about their relationship, it was a fantasy of her servitude. "You will never seem as beautiful as when I see you roll up your sleeves and work for me. We could be so happy. You would fall behind in your writing!"[6] For Henry Miller, Nin's denial of herself was validation of his own importance. He only revealed his own chauvinism in his peculiar notions of what made her beautiful and happy.

Nin described that loss of self, the loss of boundaries, the rush of losing one's head which characterises romance:

"Everything is secondary to Henry... My journal writing breaks down, because it was an intimacy with myself. Now it is interrupted constantly by Henry's voice, his hand on my knee." But, having recognised Henry as a hindrance to intimacy with herself, Nin soon realised that romance offered no resolution to the divisions she felt inside; rather it accentuated them. She confesses to her journal that she still felt "alone and divided". Soon afterwards she was able to allow herself to consider for a moment "a world without Henry" and imagined doing away with the romantic in herself: "I will kill my vulnerability... by the most frenzied debauch."[7]

Nin's new fantasy was of becoming "shameless, strong, sure of my actions, refusing to be impressed by others". At some point, perhaps when her work was belittled by Miller, Nin found sufficient consciousness to resist further romanticisation of a relationship in which she was the sacrificial lamb. Perhaps it was a night like the night I received the message to phone Evan "now" – to disregard my sleep and my work and anything else I might need in order to see to him.

Her romance with Miller over, Nin found that her "image of a sensual, dynamic Henry is gone... I realise... that his insecurity is equal to mine, my poor Henry." She went to Henry now "without joy", afraid of encountering "a gentle Henry... too much like myself". She marvelled at the fact that she had once risked marriage and happiness "to sleep with Henry's letter under my pillow, with my hand on it".[8]

The long-running conflict for Nin was in wanting to be faithful, but also wanting to experience life: "I crave to love wholly... Yet I am driven by diabolical forces outside of all grooves." After having tried to live within the model, Nin rebelled against the narrow simplicity of the good girl–bad girl dichotomy, preferring a more complicated morality which valued "the ultimate loyalty and overlooks the immediate and literal one". She understood that her first loyalty needed to be to herself, wherever that might take her and despite the fact that the path to selfhood was full of detours, including, sometimes, a return to old and tired romantic patterns. But when her own experiences finally led her to lose faith in romance, Nin felt better able to love profoundly, and humanly.

Nin's experiences underline the main problem of romanticism – its lack of humanity. Romance denies the humanity of each of us as individuals by suggesting that we require completion in another. Every human being is born complete in her or himself, but romance denies this and, from that basic denial, makes a fetish of coupling and an obsession of love. Its seductive rush is very different from the steady well-being of profoundly human love. It is an invention, a deception, and a cause of much disappointment. We might like to expect all of our lives to be as full of interest and intensity as that moment of discovering a mutual attraction. We might like every discussion to be as feverish as the first nervous exchange when we discover common interests and aspirations. But, unlike romance, real life and profound love are full of many ordinary moments.

It might seem the easy option to carry on being addicted to the rush of romance, trying to replicate its highs. Perhaps it would be easy to say our problems have stemmed from particular relationships and go on to try for better luck the next time. Anaïs Nin did carry on in this manner, but only traded the unreality of her domestic life and the isolation she felt as a suburban housewife for a different kind of romantic unreality. She wrote that she did not want to see that she was "nowhere, without friends or literary work".[9] She felt herself melting into her coquettishness, her desire to please, her seductive poses. Her need to seduce, charm and conquer was an attempt to fill her inner emptiness.

The problems we find in our involvements are not simply by-products of these relationships, but signs of personal needs, compounded by romantic illusion and exacerbated by the rigidity of our gender roles. While Nin relied on romantic diversions to make her feel the satisfaction she could not generate from within, the fulfilment she attained was short-lived, as romantic solutions usually are. Those few false, frozen moments were certainly not the times when Nin felt most herself. On the contrary, she wrote that at those moments she felt "like the very child-woman I most despise... dreadfully amused by all my little triumphs". She felt special "when I am thinking and seeing through myself and through other women; and when I am writing and reading philosophy or conversing intelligently – which are the product of Mind accidentally located in a feminine envelope."[10]

Every feminist must work in her own way to investigate the elusive images, convenient moralities and romantic notions that have been the bases of women's choices and relationships. We must work to establish conscious ways of living, through sincerity with one's own self and one's true, deepest interests. Even when we are caught in the depths of romantic illusion, we must strive for lucidity, sincerity about our insincerities, self-consciousness. This process will not be without pain, but gradually we will begin to open our eyes. We might look back on these moments of turmoil as a kind of fermentation within. What we witness is our own evolution. There are certain things that we will never again believe, lines which will not interest us any more, gestures which will never fool us. These small lessons are broad steps towards our true selves. For women, the struggle against romantic myth becomes the struggle against every trap of women's experience, every limitation, every kind of poverty of spirit and condition.

The desire to love and be loved is only human, but too often we have fallen in love too easily and quickly. So many of us are excessively grateful for the love given us when it is our due. Our need of other people can be too great, and the anxiety stemming from this need is love's quickest killer. This anxiety has nothing to do with love. It is its antithesis, and no love can thrive under the pressure of it. When we turn to others with our own anxieties, lasting and profound love is unlikely. Feelings of inadequacy, incompleteness and insecurity cut through all naturalness and erode any potential for deeper relations. As long as something that seems like love has its source in an incompleteness of self, it can only lead to further discomfort.

I remember feeling a tremendous sense of relief each time I would finally feel myself getting over an old boyfriend or infatuation. There were not many, but there were some. And in the course of my transitions, I suppose I realised that more than one man could understand and excite me. We will not have only one opportunity for true, great love and friendship, so we can afford to relax a bit. Sometimes the potential for love will be there. Sometimes it will not. Not every encounter will be profound. It is realistic and liberating to understand that some relationships might only offer experience, while others will bring deeper meanings. This is life, not romance.

We need to minimise our pain and suffering. Our liberation is in being able to enjoy our experiences without being enslaved by them.

If true, profound love is going to occur at all, it is most likely to occur when we do not feel a need to seduce. In real love, you do not want to win someone over or aim to change them, but only to understand and be understood. In real love, you do not simply focus on your want for another person, but on what is best for them. This is why we can only really love when we have enough confidence in ourselves not to need to. When you could live without someone, but don't want to – this is real free will. This is when we might choose to love. To know that you could walk away, but not want to, is where profound love might be found.

Gloria Steinem has thrown the question open to us – in a world free of romantic illusion, "Where will that 'rush' of excitement come from? Who will we become?"[11] I know that when I worked my way through and out of the illusions of romance, I felt incredibly light and free. What good and obvious news it was to really know and feel that I am complete in and of myself. I am lovable, without the perversions and contortions of seduction. This realisation brought a greater excitement than any I had ever felt through romance. And this rush of self-esteem is just as addictive as the romantic sort. Once I believed in myself in one situation, I could stand up for myself and speak for myself again, and again, and again. The inner voice has become more articulate, more opinionated, a greater and more dependable resource than anything outside of my own self could ever be.

Now I can walk through this world, never perfect, but

complete and whole in myself; confident of my intuition, open to love, but not wanting to conquer or be conquered. I have fewer fears and fewer defenses. No one can own me, and I do not require anyone else. I appreciate the humanity in myself and can recognise it in others. I have hopes for this human life, not for a romantic one. After all, what do we really give up in passing up romance? Only the anxiety of partial relationships with partial selves. Profound love includes our various selves; it does not subsume us. This is why feminist playwright Clare Boothe Luce declared that "With the equality of the sexes, there will be a lot more love in the world." More love, less romance.

Of course, no one can live an absolutely lucid life, always actively conscious. Even as we strive to be lucid and free of illusions, we will still make mistakes and some of them will be in our romances and relationships. We must live passionately, taking risks when something seems right. And it is only right to remember, too, that if there are any good, important and correct aspects of the feminine romantic role, the most important has to be our acute appreciation of the potential for emotional depth in our relationships. If the restriction of our lives to the personal realm has refined in us qualities which men have had to suppress in the competitive world, we should not now concede them. We should not compromise or abandon our hope for true communion with other human beings. But the big theme of love need not be a tragic one any longer. We will not drink iodine or put our heads in gas ovens when we feel "nobody loves me". When we do begin to feel the magnetic pull of romance, we will learn to possess the feminist insight to ask, Why?

The Usual Poses

FEMINISM CAN NOW inform our understanding that men and women have placed impossible demands upon each other and on the very notion of relationship. In the course of this, women have become too passive, and men and women alike have become confused, resentful, envious and removed from qualities associated with the opposite sex. Gloria Steinem believes that the resolution of our rifts and recovery of our true selves will require not only identification and empathy for the predicaments of the opposite sex, but a certain measure of androgyny. She emphasises that such recovery will probably require going against – and thus help to change – most of our romantic culture.[1]

The consequences of a strict gender-role dichotomy are always most painfully felt in our intimate relations with each other. Women are socialised in the language of emotions, but men are rarely practiced in the kinds of communication required to maintain relationships and reap the full rewards of the human connection between the sexes. Even for the sensitive "new man", identification with other men is still the main emphasis. In really cynical moments, any of us might say that male bonding is all that we've ever had.

We might have thought that man would turn to woman to draw lessons from her emotional eloquence, but for any man interested in that possibility, the social penalties and taboos of identifying with woman are considerable. Gender distinctions remain extremely rigid at the suggestion of men deviating from masculine norms or becoming at all "like a woman".

Even when identification across sexes has been tolerated in the recognition of the importance of the father-daughter relationship, there has been "no parallel emphasis on men connecting intellectually with their mothers".[2] Men are not encouraged to understand their mothers' interests and predicaments, nor to project themselves far enough to empathise with their mothers and mothers' roles. Perhaps this is not surprising in male-dominated society, where masculine traits are more valued than feminine ones. At the point of the mother-son relationship, the gender dichotomy remains firmly entrenched and almost impossible to negotiate, while controversy abounds to reinforce it. The man who does not reject femininity (and mother) in defining his own masculinity, or anyone who approaches the image of a "momma's boy", is held up to close scrutiny and suspicion as to his actual gender identification.

Not only improved understanding between men and women, but a fuller appreciation of the range of men's qualities may depend on the crucial event of man identifying with mother. This important intellectual connection, which has been the subject of so much taboo and too many Freudian hangovers, might be the relationship by which to resolve many of our sexual conflicts. Perhaps the fact that men have had to deny and repress their connection to mother and have been made to think it something perverse and distorted can explain much of the distance between men and women in a wide range of our relations. Perhaps the repression of men's connection to the wholeness of mother – her mind and soul, and the comfort once derived from the warmth and softness of her body – explains something of men's wider dismemberment and depersonalisation of women.

Sociologist Nancy Chodorow believes that "the very fact of being mothered by a woman generates in men conflicts over masculinity."[3] This is so only because of the rigidity of the gender-role dichotomy. By defining masculinity in opposition to femininity – not as sets of differences, but as two distinct poles – western cultures perpetuate man's emotional distance from mother and women in general.

Every day I try to raise my sons in ways that will not ever suggest that their maturation requires denial or rejection of me or of "feminine" qualities. I hope that each day I do inform my sons – in hundreds of ways – about all and any aspects of myself that are relevant to them. It is vital that I offer them enough of my own diversity and complexity so that they can find aspects to identify with, to incorporate into themselves and to take with them into their relationships with the women, men, mothers and fathers of our future. Let my sons realise, long before they are parents themselves, that parenting is a role, not a whole life, for men and for women. And let them also realise that we all do the best that we can in any of our roles, up to the point that our roles do not require us to deny vital parts of ourselves.

Motherhood, formerly the only role in which women could achieve a sense of control or fulfilment, should always have been seen in proper feminist perspective as an aspect, dimension and stage of life, but not a life in itself. In 1963 Betty Friedan pointed out that perpetuation of the feminine mystique is only accomplished through adherence to it by the "self-sacrificing" mother.[4] Mothers cannot become the positive and strong role models their daughters need and sons can embrace until we change our own lives and the institution of motherhood itself. In every way that we become more aware of potentials for shared and egalitarian parenting, we contribute to an expanded range of experiences and abilities for both our sons and daughters. A parent could do no greater good. My husband and I have now become accustomed to trading, bargaining and negotiating all of the smaller and larger tasks (and pleasures) that amount to parenting. Any and all of it could begin to feel like an oppressive commitment − an indefinite sentence, with no time off for good behaviour − if it were the exclusive role of one person.

Certainly we have not perfected the negotiation of parenting. I am the first to acknowledge, and to feel the effects of, our imperfect system: when something is left undone, it usually does fall to me. And I realise that all of our attempts are private measures with certain limitations. We are not affecting legislation today, and are not having an impact on this week's council agenda. It is reasonable for feminists to doubt that the voluntary actions of individuals can create fundamental social change. Structural, legal mechanisms to enforce and assist progressive change *are* vital. But we must not underestimate the significance of challenging the hegemony that has prevailed in our own homes. Patriarchy is preserved and reinforced within the family, in the domestic realm. In every way that liberal and radical feminists emphasise the tremendous range and flexibility of the family and family life, we challenge conservative hegemony at its core. It would be wrong and short-sighted to deny the power women have to change things in our most obvious, traditional domain. And it may be truly revolutionary for women to exercise that power.

I was raised in a household that seemed "feminist" by definition; my mother raised me on her own from the time I was nine and I was surrounded by sisters. But six women in a house turn feminism into a matter of shades of personality and style. If there was a struggle for definition of self, there was little to struggle against except the personalities of other women. Feminism must have been so much contained in matters of personal ambitions and talents that I was not really aware of it *per se*. Even in a household full of some of the most gifted women I have ever met or had the pleasure to know, it would seem that consciousness of feminism ceased to exist because of the absence of contrasting patriarchy.

Similarly, in the larger feminist sphere, the fact that generations of women before us have gone so far in diminishing and changing patriarchy means that young women today are able to pursue their own directions in a friendlier atmosphere. As a result, many young women have not yet felt or experienced feminist "struggle". Many are part of an educated, middle- and upper-class élite whose class privileges have given them a kind of confidence. Their real experiences of success in university and the professional world have reinforced this confidence. They do not feel invisible or barred; on the contrary, they feel personally empowered, successful and ambitious. They are proud of their womanhood and their success, and equate this sense of pride and "power" with that of feminist consciousness.

Feminist writer Katie Roiphe puts this "power feminism" in terms anyone can understand: "Feminism should be about women being successful and powerful." But there is more to feminism than that, of course. I believe that even the most conservative women will feel their feminism mature and broaden as it is tested by their own life experiences, and this will be a vital, enriching process. After all, among privileged women is where feminism started, women who resented barriers and were confident and angry enough to reject them and knock them down. We have to remember that even the feminists of "counter-revolutionary" or "neo-conservative" strains are women who call themselves feminists for the good reason that they have confidence in the system of legal and social changes which has given women a better chance to achieve a certain measure of individual success. At this moment in feminism, we need to be generous to each other. And we can afford to be enthusiastic about young women's potential for radicalisation, once we become comfortable with the idea that our most intense feminist lessons are ahead of us.

As Gloria Steinem pointed out in her insightful essay "Why Young Women Are More Conservative," women often do not feel the urgency to challenge the politics of their lives until

they have passed their youth. The stereotypes of "brave exploring youth and cowardly conservative old age" do not hold for
us. Young women are still full of the uncertainties and personal
conservatism that come with wanting to succeed and win
approval. Steinem has suggested that even if young women do
identify with the "feminist" label because they have been able
to appreciate the real progress that feminism has brought, or
because it fits in with some enlightened self-image, young
feminists are likely to "feel and behave a little like a classical
immigrant group... determined to prove ourselves" because
we "haven't yet experienced the life events that are most radi-
calising for women: entering the paid-labour force and
discovering how women are treated there; marrying and finding out that it is not yet an equal partnership; having children
and discovering who is responsible for them and who is not;
and aging, still a greater penalty for women than for men."[5]

It is in this context that I understand why young feminists
have become feminism's greatest critics and have been so
quick to see aspects of feminism as being "anti-men" or "anti-
sex". More than that, I can understand Naomi Wolf's wish to
counter some of the women's movement's antagonism to men
by defending them, their vibrancy and individuality, and the
centrality of men in women's lives. I can even almost understand how Camille Paglia's revisionist tones can begin to
sound like the "exasperated voice of common sense".[6]

It is true that much of the feminist thought we draw upon
today took its lead from what was, initially, real personal anger.
Understanding that many things which had been considered
"personal matters" were also political issues, women of the
1960s and '70s began to analyse the frustration they felt with

men and patriarchal social structures in political terms. However, women's rage only became feminism when its root causes were traced, understood and attributed to a repressive system of gender roles which goes beyond men and encompasses them. First there was anger.

Anger is hard for us to deal with, or even recognise in ourselves. It runs counter to the docile "feminine mystique" to feel and be angry. We are supposed to be content. There is no room within our mystique for the "castration lists" that Katie Roiphe refers to in *The Morning After*. I remember those lists myself, written on the walls of women's bathroom stalls at the universities I attended. When I saw them, I wasn't sure where to place them in my view of feminism. They were not helpful. And since I was not much of a feminist at the time anyway, it was pretty easy for me to see these slogans as reinforcing the image of "angry" and even "flaming" feminists. This, of course, is the image of feminism that has been suggested to young women by patriarchal elements of society, which for their own perpetuation must always marginalise feminism. And it is true, I think, that unreconciled anger is what causes us to overstate and damage our case – perhaps even marginalise ourselves. If anger expresses itself in aggression, it only mimics traditional, masculine methods and will alienate many people.

To avoid these pitfalls, we do need the ideas and vibrancy that thoughtful internal criticism can inject. Unfortunately, Katie Roiphe, Camille Paglia and Naomi Wolf have all attempted to diagnose feminism's criticism of patriarchal relations as evidence of a "victim-mentality" and concordant obsession with sexually predatory men.[7] They have attempted to trace the roots of this cowering feminism to nineteenth-century Victorianism and its notions of feminine passivity and purity, but their analyses overlook the larger context of our sexual politics and sexual mores.

Katie Roiphe argues that women – particularly feminists – have become consumed and paralysed by an awareness and dread of rape. She accuses feminists of using scare tactics by exaggerating our risks and forcing a broadening of the definition of rape to include "bad sex". But in focusing on rape Roiphe is plucking out just one element of a whole system of sexual mores that is oppressive in its tendency to idealise women on the one hand and patronise and degrade us on the other.

It was not feminism which cut women off from human qualities and desires. It was not feminism which portrayed women as either mystical or savage, and sex as mysterious and threatening. It was, rather, romantic ideology. The nineteenth-century gender etiquette which has so defined our roles to this day (and was perhaps itself defined by Queen Victoria when she vowed always to act as her husband Albert would have wished) was marked by a deeply conservative morality which separated ideal spiritual qualities in women from "base" human characteristics. Such romanticism, reflected in art, philosophy and broader social attitudes, has always denied the wholeness of women, and left us perched precariously between the extremes of idol and object. We need to consider the effects of romanticism before concluding that feminism has de-sexed society or made us all neuter, as Camille Paglia has argued. If we want to understand and not simply find fault with the fact that women have felt real rage towards men and have, at the same time, felt hateful and defensive of their own bodies and physical being, then we need to look at how the culture of romance has so divided women from their real selves. Without a feminist analysis of this kind, it's little wonder that attaining a sense of wholeness has seemed such an elusive prospect in our individual lives.

The psychological dissonance that results from the Victorian rift between woman as spiritual idol and woman as physical object is difficult for both women and men to bear. Women have been made to repress and deny their sexual essence and physical reality; men have tried, with difficulty, to separate sex from feeling. Rape fantasies are the expressions of both men's need to separate their feelings and women's desire to separate their reputations from the physical act of sex. Another expression of this dissonance is the tendency for men to separate women into the sort to marry and the sort to go to bed with. The phenomenon of the man who is no longer interested in a woman once he has "got her" becomes less mysterious when we understand the repression and dissonance imposed upon us all.

Where, as a society, we are not comfortable with the feminist ideal of equals freely choosing to enter physical and emotional relationships, we can see phenomenal numbers of men seeming simply to be "unable to make a commitment". When a man does make a commitment, it might still be a matter of having been "cajoled", finally giving in to the social pressure to "do right by her" and "make an honest woman of her". For such men, the greatest threat is the woman who would have him.

In the Victorian scheme of sexual mores, when women consented to sex, it was meant to be confined to legal, heterosexual relationships. Separating physical indulgence from the sanctity of formal commitment was looked upon as deviant. Even today, when sexual experimentation is practiced, sex is still not considered legitimate for women unless we also employ the rhetoric of "love". This saves our reputations by showing that our intentions are pure. We remain virtuous.

Social scientist Philip Slater argues, "The idea that pleasure could be an end in itself is so startling and so threatening to the structure of our society, that the mere possibility of it is denied."[8] Many men have thought the resolution of our sexual inhibitions would be found in freeing sex from emotional attachments and expanding the principle of "free sex". In this they have failed to realise that promoting the separation of the physical and the emotional only reinforces the central Victorian ethic that these two vital aspects of the feminine condition cannot be reconciled. While such Victorian mores are unchallenged, emphasis upon the purely physical aspects of sex remains, for women, an illusion of sexual liberation.

For too long women's behaviour has been portrayed in terms of the good girl–bad girl dichotomy, with the major choices of our lives cast between "virtue" and experience, between traditional passivity and our assertion of our own interests. We have faced difficult decisions, constantly drawn along the wrong lines. The ways in which these false distinctions can drive women to despair were never better illustrated than by Anaïs Nin in the volume of her journals entitled *Henry and June*. She writes of her life becoming "deformed" as her attraction to Henry Miller struck at "the centre of the most perfect, the most steadfast structure, marriage. When this shakes, then my whole life crumbles." But in the midst of this chaos, things seemed to be "turning out badly", not because of intentional evil or malice, but because of the sort of imbalance which makes "even the most cherishable and sacred things seem so illusory, unstable, transitory".[9]

Nin still felt devoted to her husband, but had become distracted: "I have always been attached to him ideally. I am now, but not sensually. There is another man, a more animal man, who really holds me strongly." Even so, she panics for the familiar comfort of her husband and admits to herself: "I am definitely ill. My mind is not altogether in power." She thought she had exhausted her capacity for tragedy in romance, but again found that the perversity of being made to choose between the virtue of marriage and the experience of a full life drove her to confront the restrictions she had become accustomed to and to imagine another, larger existence.[10]

Having played the good daughter and good wife and found both roles closing in on her, Nin saw her only other option at the other extreme of the female dichotomy. If she was not content with the traditional roles, she imagined that she must be "bad". She set out to "build a new shell, wear new costumes". Yet nothing quite fit. She wrote of a new manner she constructed for herself, "seductive, affable, gay, and within this I am hidden". Surely this begins to sound familiar to many of us. Nin began to hide behind seduction and promiscuity, guises for her own insecurities and an expression of her discontent with passive "virtue". She was conscious of relying upon the usual poses, but thought she would find security and independence in conquering and controlling men. She felt that she would sooner devour men than become dependent again.[11]

But did she, through all of this supposed rebellion, under-stand more about herself? Did she find independence? Did she feel secure? Or do any of us, in our flirtations? Like other dominated people, we have learned to "internalise men's will and make it ours, and men have sometimes characterised this as 'power' in us; but it is nothing more than the dependent's 'power' to disguise her feelings – even from herself – in order to obtain favours, or literally to survive."[12] Nin still felt envi-ous of other people's qualities and was uncomfortable with her own. She admitted that she only felt beautiful at moments, here and there, by a trick of clothes or expression.[13]

For women, liberation in gender relations will depend not on further dividing themselves, but on resolving the rift between the physical and the emotional aspects of our being. While the masculine definition of sexual liberation and its reinforcement of the Victorian emotional and physical rift con-tinue to dominate discourse on sexual relations, we will still find feminist critiques of rape and pornography spoken of in terms of "prudishness". Even while many women do not accept these terms, our dissatisfactions with sexual relations often remain abstractions. Some of us act out in desperate attempts to bridge our internal and external realities by simply feeling and doing, not thinking. It is a "chaos designed and planned by a game which delights ultimately in confusing the issues, destructively so... [It is] the supreme irony, for the game turns to be a game of the irrational, arranged in a supreme disarrangement..."[14]

The role of the "fallen woman" presents particular chal-lenges to prevalent Victorian sexual ethics. She is both the theme and anathema of woman labouring under the strain between mind and body, where sexual relations are functional and physical, divorced from emotion and reason. This "fallen" woman, having known respectability through the fulfilment of her duty and gender role as a "good wife", risks her status to confront the lust and torment she feels inside. Fascination with this figure reveals societal fears of what she represents. The fallen woman runs head-on into all the taboos of middle-brow mass culture and confronts the old whore–madonna dichotomy. She becomes both. She has felt and responded to the incongruity of being raised on a pedestal as the image of sacred womanhood, while rarely feeling beloved or esteemed. She is Jezebel – the image of woman's discontent with Victorian double standards. By labelling her as "fallen", male-dominated society not only marginalises her as deviant but contains her discontent, and in doing so justifies the social controls placed upon all women.

Jezebel becomes just one more romantic distortion, another dismal, failed attempt to reconcile our various selves by living them out to extremes. She fulfils an empty promise as she spends much of her own time lonely and fixated – thinking about a man, wondering what a man is doing right now, focusing on a man's needs and wants and plans for the future. Rather than make her own plans, she wonders if he will see fit to include her in his.

Women who imagine "having it all" in the role of Jezebel might be, like I was, surprised at how little they find. The separation of our physical and emotional selves remains and continues to affect our relationships, while the patterns of our lives continue to betray a larger discontent. Whether we are our lover's wife or mistress, the reality for most women is that, much of the time, we find ourselves left "begging for more".

If we can begin to understand and view our discontent in a politicised way, we might not resort to the desperate, individual rebellions that amount to little more than snatching at love and do nothing to address the emptiness we feel. But it is up to us to realise that we have been begging for the things we must define for ourselves. Women must begin to form the feminist analyses which will lead us to new sexual ethics and an expanded view of gender relations, with an emphasis upon "big love" and not simply "free sex". Toward this, Adrienne Rich has suggested a redefinition of female "honour" – no longer cast in terms of Victorian values of virginity, chastity, and fidelity to a husband, but based on the timeless virtue of honesty among women.[15]

For now, romanticism remains. It is here and now. It has never left us. How wrong it has been to blame feminists themselves for endowing sex with some sort of lurking, threatening qualities that they supposedly "invented". How naïve even to imagine that feminists have that sort of social authority over sex, a fantasy that has led directly to the insulting portrayal of women's "victimhood" as something we have chosen for ourselves and exploited. The idea that we have adopted and begun to incorporate into ourselves a notion of victimhood is a dangerous distraction to progressive feminism, but much more insidious is the fact that this victimhood fits so well with the learned passivity of women. This dangerous combination could plant the sorts of internal doubts that diminish our confidence in our own ability to judge and analyse our life experiences.

Conservative feminists have effectively undermined the rest of us by suggesting we speak and act out of some sort of pathological attraction to an heroicised status of the victim. Through the peculiar logic of neo-conservative feminists, the fact that we have been oppressed and have been able to recognise our oppression as such is our new illness, our pathology, our neurosis. The only way to counter this distorted logic is through constant awareness and analysis of our own predicaments. Perhaps through the "virtue of honesty" in our personal difficulties, and through the sharing of solutions, we can remain focused on understanding our responsibilities to ourselves and to one another.

Reinventing Womanhood

SOCIAL THEORIST WALTER Lippman wrote: "The discontent that is shocking the world cannot be dealt with by politics only, or on the periphery of life, but must touch the central and intimate places of personal life." The discovery of true confidence does not take place in the political realm, but deep within the self. So we must unseal the great taboo that has kept women from having their own formulations, definitions and orientations. Our liberation is in realising that the solutions to most of our crises are within, and not in a partner or change of partner. It might be difficult, at first, to face the fact that there are no masculine quick-fixes to our predicaments, but in realising our own responsibilities here, we place the power for defining ourselves in the right place. By involving ourselves, we create the potential for self-emancipation. There is no trace of victimhood in this truly conscious feminism of self.

Having pursued the legal and structural work that must be done, and considered the interpersonal changes that we require in the home and workplace, feminists must now delve deeply into woman's inner world. If we are to escape the external illusions that have too long formed our behaviour and determined our decisions, we must search for security and sincerity within. This, I believe, is the work of the third wave of feminism.

Our culture has placed a tremendous taboo on women's introspection, on the notion of finding purpose and meaning within our own selves. And that is also why, I think, we have sometimes resorted to success on men's terms, trying to be the best men we can be, to fight fire with fire. However, this is a mechanical way to empowerment and a tragic way to attain meaning and achievement. We are only identifying with a different aspect of the same oppressive system of gender roles that has limited women's and men's lives when we fail to work toward any sort of more significant transformation of both genders. In this respect, the strictly political and careerist "power" feminism has provided an important but unfortunately narrow response to a broad problem. We have lost much of the transcendent call embedded in feminism and have failed to appreciate the fact that politics alone will not solve the crises of women's selves.

But how difficult it is for woman to develop a psychology of her own when she constantly lives under the deeply-ingrained habit of placing others' needs before hers. As Gloria Steinem wrote in *Revolution From Within*, "many of the personality traits holding us back are seen as inherent in females. If self-sacrifice, a lack of personal will, living through others, fear of confrontation, and a need for approval are considered part of women's 'natural' self, there isn't much reason to search for other causes."[1]

The crux of our predicament, then, is that in order to achieve self-discovery we must undertake a process of deconstructing the images of our former selves and reinvent our womanhood. Not an easy task on the best of days, this is much more difficult on days when the walls of our homes seem to be closing in or falling down, but there is no opting out of this process once you reach the end of your ability to function according to old patterns.

Gloria Steinem tells how she simply could no longer cope in the ways to which she had become accustomed: "I had come to the burnt out end of my ability to travel one kind of feverish, productive, but entirely externalised road – and I had no idea why." She began to suffer a "profound feeling of depression" which she had not even defined as such. Desperate for some sense of balance, she had to find a way to function, other than by the sort of personal crisis management she had survived on. She writes that she began to understand why she was "co-dependent with the world". "I was so moved by anyone whose plight seemed invisible. Carried over from my own childhood – and redoubled by growing up with the invisibility of a female in a male-run society – my sympathy reflected my own feelings of nonexistence. I had retreated to researching and reporting because I doubted the reality of my inner voice."[2]

Only a few years ago, when I was still in school, succeeding

at university and at the peak of my value to men as a potential wife, mother, and worker, I always felt like I was pulling
off some kind of a hoax. I did very well in school, well enough
for my achievements to be recognised by a couple of the best
universities in the world. I had some good friends and an
interesting, supportive family. Still, I could not make myself
feel real. Instead of feeling confident and taking each success
as verification of my abilities, I really thought I was a fake who
had been merely lucky. I believed so little in the reality of my
own efforts that I felt like I was doing nothing. I felt every
achievement as part of a larger bluff and feared that my true,
inner "nothingness" might be found out at any time. It was a
time in my life when I was really living for myself, contributing to and building my own future, but I saw no value in all
this. I walked around in emptiness. With every encounter, I
felt a kind of artificiality of my own self. Whatever people
thought of me and however impressed they seemed or kind
they were, I felt they only responded to an image of me and
had been convinced by something I had only just managed
to pull off.

I can remember waiting to feel grown-up and supposing
that a sense of myself would come with that. But I never felt
grown-up. I waited, but even after I had managed to form an
important relationship with Liam, and after I was married, I
still felt very small and unreal. According to the traditional
scheme of women becoming significant when they are of use
to other people, I should have felt more substantive with
Liam. But in not seeming to want to spend time with me,
Liam also seemed not to need me. I continued feeling without purpose and without substance. In the midst of my

romantic affair with Evan, even though I was flattered and relieved to feel wanted, I thought he too had probably been attracted to a false impression of me. I try to make sense of the feeling I had through those years. I think that perhaps I was caught in some kind of a void between the false selves that my culture had suggested to me as a woman and the true self which I missed and, often, grieved for. Within me there remained an undeniable quietness that I could neither escape nor overcome.

I may have considered myself a feminist at times, but like many of the women of my generation, my attachment to feminism was a bit uncertain. I had a kind of soft focus, a diffuse sense of what feminism was and almost no sense of what it was supposed to mean to me. I had the intellectual grasp of it – had read the journal articles, attended the lectures, even joined a round-table discussion group - but I did not know exactly how feminism would take on a relevance in my own life. I knew that I was being afforded opportunities in education that were denied women a decade before. I knew that I had a certain freedom of outlook to imagine my future from a vast range of possibilities, opened to me only by the struggles of generations of women before me. And yet, as much as I tried to talk the talk and walk the walk, I could not articulate a feminist perspective in any way that felt personally relevant. It was as though equality was important because... "Well, equality is a good thing." You see? It just didn't mean anything.

Then, and now, some of the women of my generation would say that feminism and the women's movement were things that had "happened", special events which had taken place and were now over. In company where it was unfashionable to be a feminist – whenever it was thought of as "cold" or "angry" – I was right there with an apology to precede any feminist statement I might make: "I'm not a feminist or anything, but..."

At school and at home, in thousands of spoken and unspoken ways, I had absorbed lots of important feminist information. These principles – at the same time modest and radical – were essential to me, at the threshold of a generation of uncertain feminists. I learned that women are entitled to the hopes and dreams to which we aspire. I understood our aspirations for success, fulfilment and security are not particularly masculine or feminine, but human. Above all else, I began to get the message that it is wrong and sometimes dangerous for a woman to expect a man to build the world she wants. But it is one thing to hear all of this, to say it or to write it. Quite another to live it.

With all that I seemed to know, I hardly realised that I did not yet know how to live a conscious life, free of illusion. I really did not know what was inside of me. It was not enough to be told that I was as good as any man. I didn't know what men were about either. I think that those early feminist lessons did help me identify patriarchy when I felt it, did reassure me that my frustrations were real, and suggested that anger is appropriate at times. But the feminism I had encountered remained weak when it came to helping young women like myself discover what would make us happy or bring us success on our own terms. Perhaps we still lacked the confidence to envision the future of women, distinct from men and with our own criteria.

A popular criticism of feminism to this point has been that it is too focused on criticising the present, too defensive, too reactive. Gloria Steinem acknowledged that "feminist writers and theorists tend to avoid the future by lavishing all our analytical abilities on what's wrong with the present, or on revisions of history and critiques of the influential male thinkers of the past. The big, original, and certainly courageous books of this second wave of feminism have been more diagnostic than prescriptive."[3]

By not having focused on defining success on our own terms or even questioning what men consider success to be, many women have tended to fall back on and adopt masculine definitions of achievement. Not only have we largely accepted the idea of success being something we can realise in the workplace, but we have also begun to measure self-worth in terms of financial mobility, career advancement, and the ability to "juggle". Did success by men's standards come more easily to us than we imagined it would? We had developed the chameleon flexibility to be so many things to so many people that sometimes we found ourselves as good at being like men as men are. We merely took our self-sacrificial devotion to duty and our tendency to live for others to the workplace, where they looked like super-competence.

Much of feminism to date has focused on the professional potential of women. With so much thought dedicated to aspects of and obstacles to women's success at work, a lot of feminist theory has been reduced to important, but limited, arguments of style: developing confidence and assertiveness, our potential as mediators, the practicalities of cooperation, opportunities presented by networking. In many ways we have worked more towards applying ourselves and our "feminine" qualities to the workplace than to challenging the very definition of "success" for both genders.

There is no denying that some of the evidence of women's success – even on "men's terms" – is staggering. Yet while courageous and ambitious female pioneers in medicine, law, business and politics may attain celebrity-like status, far less attention has been paid to the concessions "successful" women are required to make. While marriage and children are considered vital aspects of the "stability" and "balance" of male executive life, most women in senior management are not married and most do not have children. Though a family is considered an asset for men in politics, women candidates are exposed to subtle criticism for neglecting their households, husbands and children.[4]

The woman who succeeds at work is also subject to the invidious stereotyping, harassment and constant, sharp criticism contained in doubts as to the "real reasons" for her success. Gloria Steinem found it ironic that, after a lifetime of work to combat these elements, she is thought of as "the pretty one", the acceptable face of feminism. I will take the risk of sounding "angry" and "defensive" in saying that there is, in that, a kind of diminishment of her work. If she cannot be co-opted or defused in any other way, she can be considered, primarily, pretty.

Because the definition of success for the sexes has had everything to do with giving form and assigning function to our gender roles, challenging it would go a long way in opposing patriarchy and freeing both women and men from the rigidity of our roles. For now, while we continue to be satisfied with success on men's terms, we have been co-opted. Feminism has been effectively incorporated into the individualism of the status quo. Patriarchy remains essentially unthreatened. It is on this account that conservatives have no trouble mouthing the suggestion that the women's movement has "won". All of this fits perfectly into the conservative framework: if feminism has succeeded, now the only barriers to political and economic achievement are individual shortcomings. In other words, our status is certainly not society's problem – indeed, not even a "woman's issue" any longer, but simply "her problem".

For too long feminism has almost exclusively depended on the idea that it was the denial of paid work outside of the home – this "waste of human talents" – that had traumatised women and created intolerable dependencies. During the 1960s, '70s and '80s, feminism relied heavily on the argument that without paid and recognised work, women lose self-respect and "our ability to prove that we are alive by making some difference in the world". Betty Friedan emphasised the "solution" of paid work as a chance for women to pursue prestige and power in the ways that men always have.[5] We had not even questioned the validity of these standards of "fulfilment" for men before adopting them for ourselves.

There is no doubt of the importance and necessity of paid work, but the feminist movement's emphasis on work as a gateway to freedom has invested work with a kind of significance that many working women themselves could not divine. This glorification of the workplace overlooked the drudgery and sheer necessity of paid work in many women's lives, just as it seemed to exclude housewives and the unemployed and prevented them from identifying with feminism. Of course, employment equality has been significant to the progress of the women's movement. Feminist historian Rochelle Gatlin considers the pivotal role performed by working women in the midst of the conservative climate of the 1950s. Though they may not have seen themselves as feminists, these women functioned as "the literal and metaphoric mothers of the women's movement... [posing] possibilities for political change denied to homemakers. Paid work, even in the most stereotyped 'women's jobs', differed from work at home; measurable rewards, clearly set hours of labour, and companionship with peers were found at most workplaces."[6]

Indeed, it is the camaraderie among women that sometimes can keep us in jobs that have few other redeeming qualities and little financial incentive. Work is, among other things, a reason to get together, an opportunity for prolonged and sustained contact with other women. Still, for the most part, work itself has not been the deliverance many feminists professed it would be. In studying women's sense of identity and self at middle-age, sociologist Lillian Rubin found that work boiled down mainly to a pay-cheque – not to happiness, success or fulfilment. According to Rubin's findings, most women do not identify themselves primarily in terms of their jobs. Rubin found this to be true, whether or not the women's jobs were high-level "meaningful" jobs or less glorified work. Many radical and socialist feminists have emphasised the alienating nature of work under capitalism, and pointed out the futility of seeking fulfilment in this way. However, this radical emphasis on alienation has often seemed to run counter to the task of building women's sense of empowerment and self worth, and so the women's movement has tended to emphasise pragmatic issues like the importance of equality of pay and employment opportunities.

Certainly the liberal strains of the women's movement have been successful in addressing the obvious legal, social and economic impediments to the lives of women. Even if sexual equality is rarely achieved as a fact, it is now almost universally accepted as a goal. In the decades since World War II, many countries have revised their family codes, marriage laws and divorce laws in view of a new, enlightened understanding of women's rights and needs. And while women may not find it easy or even possible to get access to well-paid, high-skill jobs, the principle of equal pay for work of equal value has been widely accepted and ratified in the International Labour Office's Equal Remuneration Convention of 1951 and Article 19 of the European Economic Community's Treaty of Rome.

Up until 1963 it was legal in the US to pay women less than men for the same work. Beginning in 1966, the National Organisation for Women (NOW) committed itself not only to securing equal pay legislation in the U.S. but enforcing its practice, increasing employment opportunities, eliminating sex discrimination in employment practices and prosecuting cases of sexual harassment in the workplace. NOW provided a base for the first broad wave of the women's movement since the women's suffrage movement. The appeal of this second wave of women's activism was based on emphasising the logic of extending basic liberal-democratic principles to women. Central to this appeal was the understanding that equality between women and men is an integral part of the foundation of any just society.

Many young American women who came to feminism during the 1960s and '70s had been affected and influenced by their experiences in the Civil Rights Movements, New Left student activism, the Anti-Vietnam War Movement, and opposition to the Cold War. The risk and potential for danger in each of these earlier movements – even in demonstrations that were intent upon peace – fostered a kind of macho ethos, a sense of the "brotherhood of men" rather than the equality of people. Many progressive women, having had the courage to act on their intellectual interests and moral indignation, still found themselves marginalised, their talents neglected within these movements. While men debated and made plans, women were making coffee, tea and sandwiches; often typing, photocopying and stapling, but not being heard. When they did speak, they spoke to each other and became conscious of their own subordinate relationship to men. The distance between the ideals of equality that progressive movements of the 1960s espoused and the inequitable realities that women experienced within the movements, provided the social space in which discontent and anger began to form a feminist consciousness. Through the political contacts and personal friendships established within progressive movements, women began to form their own movement based on sisterhood.[7]

Experience had already shown that the fulfilment of the most basic Western political values of equal opportunity and fair play for women seemed "radical", even to many progressive minds of the Left. Still, many feminists had a kind of liberal faith that involving women in existing institutions would change the nature of institutions more than it would require any sort of compromises or "adjustments" in women's personae. In that sense, liberal feminists may have been naïve, but also hopeful and determined.

The women's movement has worked to encourage and ease the incorporation of women into society, while hoping to diminish the degree to which society has been male dominated. Its effects have been considerable and far reaching. The success of feminism's strategy of encouraging women' participation in the workforce can be measured by the increasing numbers of women making up the labour forces of the advanced, industrialised counties. With a few exceptions among relatively traditional societies like Spain and Italy, more than a third of all adult women in industrialised societies are in the labour force. In the USA, Britain, France, Germany, Eastern Europe and Scandinavia, the proportion is over half. Numbers have increased sharply since the 1950s, but the really dramatic change in virtually all industrialised countries has been the increased participation of married women. Not only does the increased workforce participation of married women include women who are mothers, but work rates for mothers have risen even faster than rates for women in general.[8] Certainly the growing social acceptance of working women and working mothers is one of the reasons for these trends.

Still, it has been argued by many radical feminists that women's increased participation in the labour force is not evidence of a new sense of empowerment or entitlement, nor related to any newly found confidence, as we might have expected or hoped. Some suggest that it has been economic inflation – which has meant that most families need two incomes – and rising divorce rates that have propelled women into the job market. Rochelle Gatlin asserts that increases in female employment are the result of basic economic necessity, along with growth in the clerical and service industries which have traditionally employed women. Gatlin points out that, more than twenty years into the women's movement, at least 80 per cent of employed women were working in occupations that had always been considered "women's work" – as secretaries, bookkeepers, teachers, waitresses and retail sales clerks. Many of these jobs have been part-time, low-wage and without benefits. Where there have been increases in women's representation in male-dominated professions and trades, Gatlin argues these increases coincide with changes toward routinisation and deskilling of these jobs.[9]

Radical feminists contend that economic necessity also explains the striking increases witnessed in the percentage of married mothers in the workplace over the last several decades. American figures, for example, show that in 1948, only 26 per cent of American mothers living with their husbands and with school-aged children were working outside of the home. By the early 1960s, 41.5 per cent of married women with school-aged children were in the work-force. In 1984, 59 per cent of married women with school-aged children were in paid work, with 70 per cent of all women with children over age six in the labour force. Women often feel a considerable amount of ambivalence and guilt in dividing their days and nights between motherwork, housework and paid employment. Despite the stress of these responsibilities, in the United States mothers' workforce participation rates have continued at about 60 per cent for married mothers and 70 per cent for all mothers through the early 1990s.[10]

In the early 1980s, when my generation was either in secondary school or not far from it, more than half of all American families depended on the salaries of both husband and wife. During the 1970s, the economic growth and improvements in living standards that had prevailed since the end of the Second World War came to a halt. Under the pressures of a shrinking economy and widening gap between the living standards of upper- and lower-class families, one income became inadequate for most families. Most women no longer had the choice of working or not working, and many of us saw our own mothers struggling with the double burden of paid employment and domestic duties. And while any working mother embodies a concept of womanhood that includes a wide range of activities, most of them worked and still work in jobs which do not suggest social mobility, "career" paths or "fulfilment".

Most women of my generation – this potential third wave – having seen our own mothers work outside the home, have expected to work in paid employment ourselves, whether or not we married or had children. Of course, jobs with higher pay and status are preferred,[11] but even in such desirable circumstances, do most women expect work *per se* to be liberating? Having witnessed my own mother working as a secretary for more than thirty years at IBM and Esso/Exxon, it didn't look like liberation to me. If young women today seem to lack interest in feminism and are not attracted to a women's movement, it may have something to do with the inordinate emphasis that feminists of the previous generation had placed on "productive, honoured work" as a "natural" part of us and "one of life's basic pleasures".[12] This has nothing to do with the real strains and ambivalence which both genders experience in paid work.

In her study of working-class women, sociologist Louise Kapp Howe writes of the "seeds of unreality" in the glorification and glamourisation of work: "So-called glamourous workers in so-called glamourous jobs will never account for more than a fraction of the workforce in our most unglamourous job market. Only 15 per cent of women are classified as professionals, and most are teachers and nurses."[13] Combining paid work and fulfilment might have seemed possible for feminists who were able to work for and find self-expression within the women's movement, but not everyone is "free enough of the 'system' to evolve an organic work life. Some jobs simply cannot be transcendentalized."[14]

Work is just work for most people. For women, often it is just "more work". Paid work has become one of the realities of women's lives, without leading to liberation or social mobility for most of us. And while there has been a broadening and diversification of women's roles outside of the home, there has been no real change in the division of labour in the domestic realm, where the genders meet most intimately and spend most of their time.

With these lessons behind us, this is the exciting moment when the greatest challenges of gender and deepest questions of liberation and fulfilment lie open to a third wave of feminists. The last decade, which has seemed to present a decline in feminist consciousness, has also been a time when feminist thought has broadened and diversified. This is a decade during which feminism has been "transformed in two important directions: increased awareness of class and race issues... and greater attention to global problems and perspectives."[15] The challenge to feminism today is not in getting the egalitarian case accepted in theory, but in getting it put into practice through the application of human solutions to human problems. Women have been applying their personal concerns and feminist values to defend a broad range of humanist principles on progressive fronts, ranging from environmental and anti-nuclear concerns to matters of the third world and community health issues. In having extended their belief in their own intrinsic worth as women to a respect for the integrity of "Mother Earth" herself and a respect for human existence in general, women have brought their own transformation of consciousness to bear on transforming the reality around them.

If you only ask whether women today are identifying themselves as feminists, the answer would undoubtedly confirm the lull that we all have sensed in feminist theory. But before we speak of a decline in feminist consciousness, we must consider that many women's understanding of feminism may have changed – not declined – and changed in vitally important ways. Women who have come to an understanding of their own internal strengths are drawing upon that strength to lead a variety of progressive movements. Women in the anti-nuclear movement are twice as likely as men to be local leaders. Most of the organisers, volunteers and contributors to third world relief agencies are women. The work of women, extending their "maternal instincts" beyond private functions toward protection of social life and the future itself, helped to bring an end to the cold war.

So while there has seemed to be an ebb in specifically feminist activism, there has been a tremendous diversification in the political activities of women. Rochelle Gatlin feels confident that "this expanded feminist agenda, incorporating peace, ecology, and social justice, revives the hope and possibility that human and other-than-human life will continue to exist and flourish on this planet".[16] This "global feminism" is the expression of the connections women have made between personal issues of empowerment and matters of institutional change. In the same ways that feminism has always meant to help women transcend difficulties, feminist-inspired global visions are providing alternatives to political despair and powerlessness.

In addition to the global feminists whose transformations are evident, there are countless other women who have changed their lives on account of feminism, without having joined a group or identified themselves as feminists. This is all part of the maturation of feminism and the women's movement. Certainly the point of our work has never been to count numbers, but to affect consciousness and tackle women's despair. Feminist intentions have not been simply to build another organisation, but to rebuild lives and develop individuals. It is difficult to know in exactly what terms we should measure the success of a long-term campaign whose accomplishments are not in the length of membership lists or sums of contributions, but in the understanding of the authentic human qualities of both women and men. In this sense, feminism is a philosophy which has not brought anything that did not exist before, but has only reminded us of the strengths within ourselves and encouraged us to apply them in our own imaginative ways. Its effects are best observed behind the eyes of women who have discovered their own graces.

The Self-Made Woman

HAVING LED A movement towards social justice, feminists have succeeded in raising political consciousness in our world, but only up to a point. Has feminism succeeded in reaching our subconscious? The subconscious refers to that emotional core that is one's inner self – perhaps the most central and most neglected component of contemporary feminism. While second-wave feminists did not want to make women feel more powerless by focusing on their alienation, women still suffered inside, psychologically. Even as all manner of social and political reform was undertaken, women's inner selves remained shrunken. We could not compensate for the diminished state of our internal selves solely with political changes. The psychological ground that had been lost to a "nature" of self-sacrifice could not be made up in terms of political gains alone.

The personal story of Gloria Steinem holds a mirror up to contemporary feminism. The course of her life provides tremendous insight into what has happened to the second wave of feminists and threatens a third. While Steinem gave herself to her career and political involvement, her deeper personal development was deferred. Twenty years into her feminism, she heard the urgent and undeniable call of an inner voice – that of a half-woman, half-created artist, half-writer and half-dancer – reminding her of the unfulfilled aspects of herself. She wrote, "It's a feeling of 'clicking in' when that self is recognised, valued, discovered, esteemed – as if we literally plug into an inner energy that is ours alone, yet connects us to everything else." Without belittling the importance of the political work to which she had dedicated so many years, Steinem recognised a need to balance the exterior and interior worlds. She began to realise that "self-esteem isn't everything; it's just that there's nothing without it".[1]

When Gloria Steinem realised that for twenty years she had never gone more than a week without getting on an airplane, that she had no time to fix and decorate her own personal space and that her apartment was more like a headquarters than a home, she began to feel the absence of her personal life. To make matters worse, she began to realise that all of the duties that surrounded her and threatened to engulf her at any moment had not been instilled by society or by her movement and associates, but were the result of an internal pressure. No one had expected her to be all things to all people. No one had expected her to do a full range of duties within the women's movement and produce a magazine for its subscribers. She had allowed this situation to develop out of her need to prove herself and believe she was in control of all aspects of her own life. Now her feminist "duties" began to present themselves as a self-imposed, internalised oppression.

Steinem has only recently realised the irony of having brought to the women's movement "the very training in self-lessness we are trying to change".[2] Unable to draw upon the energies of a shrunken and neglected inner self, Steinem was feeling the same kind of chaos and confusion that so many of us have felt in our own vague, depressed, formless inner worlds. Yet we still consider these issues strictly "personal" and fail to trace the roots of our emptiness to that training in self-lessness that does not allow the time or will for an interior life.

Just as Steinem had been disillusioned by the choice she thought had to be made between inner growth and social movement, the wider women's movement has been caught between the concept of self-development and social progress. We placed interest in personal growth in opposition to commitment to social justice, without realising that personal growth could not take anything away from the group and would have enhanced it. Having made the false distinction between the neediness of our inner selves and our require-ments for social progress, feminists of the second wave felt it was, somehow, more important to focus on the obvious and urgent external matters that needed to be changed. We are only beginning to understand the extent to which barriers exist within ourselves and stem from a deep crisis of faith and loss of confidence which no amount of political activism can secure. While the second wave of feminism has posed many of the right questions to patriarchal society, we have failed to ask ourselves some of the very personal questions that could begin to root out the patriarchy within and provide some of the more "prescriptive" answers we have needed.

When Steinem began asking herself searching questions about the relationship between her personal experience and the women's movement, she discovered many areas of her personal experience not addressed by strictly political aware-ness. But if it sounds as though feminists missed the obvious or were political only in a narrow sense, consider the fact that one of the earliest tenets of the women's movement was that of "consciousness-raising". The process of consciousness-raising – which had risen out of the progressive politics of the Civil Rights Movement, the New Left and various democra-tic students movements of the 1960s – is based on the prin-ciple that people can find a kind of liberation in talking about "personal problems" together and identifying which problems are shared on a wide scale by people in similar social circum-stances. The outcome of this narrative process is the under-standing that many so-called personal problems are collective predicaments which stem from troubled social conditions and require political action for change.

The political significance of consciousness-raising lies in the realisation that personal feelings are legitimate motives for political activism, and that, in turn, power relations are part of the most private aspects of our lives. Simply put, the "personal is political"; the quality and direction of one's life has every-thing to do with social arrangements and political conditions. In the narrative process of consciousness-raising, women can come to realise the extent of this and express their previous silences in a subtle, but deeply meaningful social and political statement. As Adrienne Rich has argued, "only the willingness to share private and sometimes painful experience can enable women to create a collective description of the world which will be truly ours".[3]

During the 1960s and 1970s radical feminists worked to make women aware of the connection between their personal predicaments and the social conditions in which they lived, and took the lead in establishing consciousness-raising as a strategy and process. But, as Rochelle Gatlin says, while the more mainstream feminists included consciousness-raising sessions in their early programmes, they viewed consciousness-raising groups with a certain amount of disdain.[4] Many feminists feared consciousness-raising would focus women's energies on personal problems rather than political issues. Feminists had already seen how subversive politics could become diffuse. The hippies of the 1960s had begun by identifying aspects of private life and tastes as political. Within the hippie subculture, women began to reject popular notions of beauty and insist that they be broadened. They created a social space in which they could feel comfortable and beautiful with hair that was not straight or blonde, noses that were not pert, and bodies that were not petite. But while the hippie subculture reflected a new awareness, that awareness was almost exclusively expressed in terms of aesthetics. As in more recent "punk" and "grunge" subcultures, in the 1960s personal lifestyle often overshadowed and substituted for any sort of coherent political agenda. Some feminists feared the same sort of diversion of their own new consciousness. They worried that they might end up talking about their personal difficulties and comforting each other, but not producing any real challenge to social and political structures.

There was a second strategic matter that caused liberal feminists to be wary of consciousness-raising. As radical feminists sought to free women from learned passivity and dependencies through a distinct women's consciousness, the process did not tend to minimise the differences between women and men – as liberal feminists had hoped – but rather sharpened them. Whether or not women's "differences" would continue to suggest "inferiority" or "weakness" to a patriarchal society was a real concern. Women in NOW, for instance, had been arguing that "the best man for a job is a woman" and demanding equality for women. They feared that to emphasise the differences between men and women, or to emphasise a new "feminine" consciousness – distinct and separate from the man's world-view – might damage the feminist argument for equality and strengthen traditional social divisions. For these strategic reasons, the idea of a strong "feminine" consciousness was played down by mainstream or liberal feminists.

In denying "feminine" consciousness, we may have lost an opportunity to broaden the very definition of what is "feminine" – to the point that today "femininity" and "feminism" are considered virtual opposites. The fact that "femininity" is not something that many women want to identify with has to be damaging to us in the deepest ways. If consciousness of our femininity were broad and deep, we might not have the problem that we do have with such terms. "Feminine" might be as acceptable and descriptive as "feminist" has become and would not be the intellectual property of conservative women. If things had been analysed slightly differently, conservatives might not be able to argue that feminists lack, insult, diminish or deny femininity. It is pretty sadly ironic that when feminists launch a direct attack on femininity, rather than the social straitjacket placed upon it, the consequence is that femininity itself seems to be a problem in need of a solution. The solution or antidote would be emasculation. The damage done by direct attacks on femininity is our own loss: loss of opportunity for women to take satisfaction, comfort and pride in being women, and the loss of opportunity to define feminism for ourselves.

But new and broader concepts of feminine consciousness are still available to us. Gloria Steinem recently asked an audience, "What ever happened to consciousness-raising?" She went on to explain: "We started out with consciousness-raising, which let us know that we weren't crazy, that the system was crazy. It was very valuable. But we've lost some of that internal personal searching and nourishment by our laundry list of issues outside... and I think we need a deeper resurgence of consciousness."[5]

When I was at university and first began to think about the role of a "feminine" or "feminist" consciousness for myself and my own life, I had only a vague notion of feminism's relevance to me. The sense that it seemed to fit in with some progressive, enlightened image that I had of myself was all I understood. My original reaction was superficial, hasty and unconvincing. There was no deep change, profound transformation or organic evolution. But while my response to feminism was shallow and ill-defined, it was through no fault of my own. I had an initial openness and responsiveness to feminism, yet no feminist message came across in a way that seemed personally relevant. I was with the spirit of feminism, but the substance seemed so far beyond me that I was lost to it. If there are other women like me, with a latent feminism and tremendous personal need, then perhaps it is time for a personally relevant concept of selfhood to be reintroduced to our understandings of sisterhood.

I needed to be deeply convinced of my own personal worth before I could even become aware of much of the oppression I experienced. Because women's self-worth has suffered under the strain of our roles and "mystique", it might be necessary for feminism to take "self" as its starting point now. Certainly my "personal feminism" did not begin with large political goals. It was only in working through acute personal crises that feminism became real to me. Now that I know and feel that I am somebody, I can think enough of myself to recognise oppression and know that it is wrong. These realisations may sound simple, but they came to me as revolutionary, even in their modesty. Awareness of my own value now helps me identify the subtleties of women's oppression and gives me the courage and motivation for a sustained, heart-felt commitment to feminism, even when feminism is derided, marginalised and simply not in vogue.

While feminists work to combat the notion that feminism has "happened" and that the women's movement is over, the popularity of a myriad of self-help therapies continues to grow, particularly among women. As much as these diverse therapies try to establish themselves as parts of a self-help or self-development movement, they lack a coherent and politicised understanding of our personal malaise. And so the most essential and basic unit of human existence, the self, is in danger of becoming another fad industry, while feminism appears as some kind of anachronism.

But we can respond to crises of the human condition in realistic, rational and politicised ways. To really know injustice, we must respect the value of our selves enough to know what an offence against self is and what it feels like. These things are not purely objective matters. Reality is how we experience, feel and see events – not events as they appear "objectively". A woman does not leave her husband because he beats her until she understands in the deepest part of her being that it is wrong for him to beat her. Through this subjective understanding, she is motivated to act. This is a political act, and it is not objective. In exactly this sense, self-development and social justice can really only work together.

In my crisis, I felt I needed to go back to the point in my personal history where I became detached from a budding, emergent sense of my own self. Perhaps it is time for the women's movement to go back in its evolution to reconnect with vital aspects of our own political education. The earliest days of the second wave of feminism – and the consciousness-raising that was too soon abandoned – provide us with clues to follow in the development of a new and vital feminism of self.[6]

One of the most influential and inspirational documents to the budding feminism of the 1960s was the Port Huron Statement of 1962, produced by Students for a Democratic Society (SDS). This document was bold enough to suggest that the language of human values was the proper language of politics. It contained references to vision, idealism and humanism. It stated that the goal of politics should be "finding a meaning in life that is personally authentic; a quality of mind ... which unites the fragmented parts of personal history", and emphasised the need for human relationships "to go beyond the partial and fragmentary bonds of function".

Radical feminists, who were interested in transforming human relationships as much as in changing social institutions, could respond to this kind of political vision. But they ran up against resistance in an unexpected place, among progressive men who drew the line of politics at the point where principles of equity might have been applied to their own relations with women. Much of the early writing of feminists shows their anger and dissatisfaction with the male leadership of the New Left and the insensitivity of these men to the unique needs and contribution of women. As women in various movements of the Left began to develop arguments and theories based on their own experiences of oppression with the men around them, they recognised the value of their own experience and began to trust their subjective perceptions of oppression. And as women told their own stories, and began to turn to each other's lives for lessons, they were engaging in the first processes of consciousness-raising.

"Because we have lived so intimately with our oppressors, in isolation from each other, we have been kept from seeing our personal suffering as a political condition," the Redstocking's manifesto declared. The manifesto went on to suggest that by exchanging personal accounts of oppressive situations, women may begin to realise that many of the situations in which they found themselves were not unique or exclusive to them, and should not be attributed to individual inadequacies.

In these ways, women did begin to understand that they were not "crazy", but that in many respects it was "the system" that was crazy. However, this is not to suggest that structural changes alone will solve the problem. To whatever degree we have internalised aspects of our own oppression, we, too, must change.

It may be difficult to recognise the internalised tyrannies; the little voices that tell us that we are not capable of doing the things we want to do; or, conversely, the oppressive, thundering echoes that tell us we must take care of everything and everyone. We must recognise that we have gone beyond the point where one half of the world is limiting the full range of the other half, to the point where women themselves have internalised and carry out socialisation in the false consciousness of gender roles. As Nin put it: "The real enemy is what we are taught, not always by man, but often by our mothers and grandmothers."[7]

Perhaps it has been most difficult to admit that some of the obstacles are within ourselves and that, through the process of internalisation, we have lost much of our self-confidence and self-esteem. Having spent too long enmeshed in the hyper-rational and super-efficient world, with its intellectualisations and generalisations, we have lost faith in our emotional intuitions, the things we know inside – the "inner teaching" that takes place through sensitivity and closeness to our subconscious selves. That is why it is extremely important now to educate each other, to reinvest our trust in our intuitions, and to inject emotional insights back into emotional problems. We can rely on each other to identify with our struggles, and to offer direction and guidance, but we must be extremely articulate at these moments.

Men – and men's ideas – have ruled the world. Men have

taught us psychology, sociology, anthropology and philosophy. Men have produced the vast majority of classics and textbooks that I will ever read. Men have seemed to be the sex that did the thinking and had the answers. Even as a little girl at mass, I saw only men read the gospel, and then go on to interpret its meaning for me in their homilies. Men were the teachers, preachers, interpreters and inventors of philosophies and religions, or so it seemed. Thinking, criticising and creating all seemed masculine traits. In a logical extension of every aspect of the gender rift, women became my models for feeling, men for thinking and doing.

Even women who are writers, creators and originators have often felt they must forsake their feminine identities and take on masculine personae. "George Sand really materialised... the real concern of the woman who starts to create and thinks that when she creates she is assuming a masculine role. George Sand... used to wear pants, and she used to smoke cigars and carry a little dagger in her waist." At the start of her career, Anaïs Nin had thought that she could only be a writer by taking on a man's name, or using only her initials. Psychoanalyst Otto Rank suggests that women's tendency to adopt male personae not only have to do with a woman's wish to make her work acceptable, but is also rooted in a belief that she is really stealing the thunder of creation from man, something she has no right to do. Consequently, the only way she can assume such creative strength is to be an imitation of man.[8]

One of Camille Paglia's loudest complaints against mainstream feminism has been that we are unable to deal with the fact that masculinity is "the most creative cultural force in history".[9] She does not go that single sound-bite further to say that this is the case because feminine creativity has been repressed and denied, and thus she contributes further to the mystification of "masculine" qualities. It is important for us to realise that the present situation has not evolved by the sheer magnificence of men and shirking ineptness of women, and that we are not condemned to maintain this status quo. That is the first important lesson we can learn. The second lesson is that we can cultivate our own creativity, not by thinking in terms of changing sexual personae or loss of femininity, but by expanding our notions of what the feminine self encompasses.

Feminism represents the social space in which women may develop their own definitions and identities. It provides the critiques we need to begin distinguishing between the false, culturally prescribed roles which have oppressed us and the true and valued aspects of femininity which we want to preserve. To complete the process, we must do away with the props, masks, anxieties and projections that have become the currency of our relating and communicating. We have spent too long making ourselves into the people whom others need us to be. Now we need to spend time with our own deepest thoughts in order to get back to our core selves and become the people we need to be.

The emphasis upon retrieving and embracing one's true self is hardly new. Most of us do hold broken and fragmented aspects of ourselves inside. We store the remnants of childhood traumas deep within, and these wounds continue to show themselves in the patterns of our lives. Therapies that centre on the "child within" encourage us to go back in memory, envision that child, relate to her, recognise her pain, love and console her for her unmet needs. This is a step toward loving ourselves, loving and forgiving others, and realising the humanity within all of us.

I considered the "child within" theory to some extent, to find some version of self that existed before I took on adult roles and before I started living for and through others. Certainly reflecting on my family and the conditions which formed me has yielded invaluable insights and an understanding of the cycles I have continued to live out in adult life. We do need to examine our pasts, particularly our childhoods, in order to understand the patterns of our relationships and the derivation of our needs. But this is just one way of discovering authentic needs and aspirations, and if it does not work for you, you are not a failure. As a woman, I have not always felt comfortable in relating to a child-like image of myself. The point is in finding the place where your emergent sense of self became stunted. If it was during childhood, go back to resolve the issues and concerns of the child inside of you. If it was when you were an adolescent or young adult, go back to that point. The child is not the only possible vision of your authentic self and is not the only means to reconnect with your unconscious needs.

When I was trying to recall my original needs and intentions, I found it most effective to identify with the young, single adult I had been after college, but before I married. It's not that I was so "together" then, but that is when I lived on my own, listened to the kinds of music I liked, took myself to the movies when I felt like it, read the books I felt like reading, and sometimes travelled around with only my backpack and sleeping bag. That was when I was forming an independent self, and I felt comfortable and satisfied in finding my way back to that incipient self, to carry on with a process that is never complete.

My separation from my husband and my move to an isolated farming community also helped me to simulate an atmosphere of youthful self-sufficiency. Left to my own devices, and in real desperation, I suppose I began my own personal therapy one night by scribbling notes on a page – not the "talking cure", but the "writing cure". I wrote because I felt that I had no one to talk to, but had to find a voice. So a journal became my listener. My notes were particularly frantic at the start. Sometimes as I wrote I also cried over the journal. I can remember watching the ink run. Sometimes the writing was that sort of "unconscious" stream of thought that comes from a deep, emotional source. I found such writing so revealing and self-instructive that I tried to find and practice methods to help me get closer to that unconscious level of thought. I would write in the mornings, straight from my sleep, before I even got out of bed. Or I would write late at night, when I was tired or over-tired. It seemed that the closer I was to my sleeping hours, the closer I was to my subconscious mode.

It was a kind of consciousness-raising that Nin initiated by releasing her own volumes of personal journals to the public. My own consciousness was raised by turning to her works and those of other conscious women. Of course, it might have been far better to have a group of conscious women to talk to, but where that does not seem possible, or when a woman is not yet ready to bring her experience to a group, worlds of books and other media do contain important insights and even some rescuing moments. Nin's understandings of the romantic world and women's subconscious are always available to me through her work. I could be reached by Nin, Gloria Steinem, Adrienne Rich, Lillian Hellman and many others in my own remote Irish kitchen. I have not known these women, but I know the feelings we have shared, and, sometimes, that is exactly the knowledge I have needed.

It was in the articulate words of other women that I found confirmation and support for my own thoughts and feelings. I could identify my problems with those of others. I could gain insight and direction from the ways other women analysed and responded to their own situations. As I was moved by their words, I gained confidence in the value of what I had to say and felt inspired to search for the voice with which to say it. In short, I started on a path toward consciousness by taking the generous leads that other women have made available to us all.

The fact that some of the blockages lie within ourselves is not a reason to despair. In taking responsibility for our situation, we can feel less helpless, knowing that the insecurities that attack us can be transformed. Many times we have been able to imagine the realisation of our greatest fears and our vulnerabilities, with little difficulty and in vivid detail, but, as Steinem emphasises, "The human mind can imagine both how to break self-esteem and how to nurture it – and imagining anything is the first step toward creating it. Believing in a true self is what allows a true self to be born."[10]

So we can begin to transcend our false socialisation and false consciousness through imagination. Right now we are capable of changing ourselves, even if we are not feeling able to change men or society. Of course, we must work for positive change at every level and in all of our relationships, but the deep changes which we make within ourselves are also bound to transform our collective life. Whatever we do to elevate our own selves will begin to transcend and permeate all of our interactions.

Even when my whole life seemed to be in a shambles, I had to imagine myself beyond that moment and believe that I would not be stuck at that point in time forever. At such critical moments, we must imagine ourselves as creative works of our own making. This, which sounds like a simple and basic notion, is radical in its strident opposition to women's helplessness, romanticism and all forms of vicarious living. At these moments our own potentials and possibilities should be our focus. This is not egocentric, but a step toward the entire world as it could be. Despair and fragmentation are choices against creativity, against the planning and designing of our own human futures. But our trials and difficulties need not be fatal. While we should never want to be less feeling, we can learn to suffer less, and not to cling to our pain, but to transcend the tragic moments.

Sylvia Plath is a prime example of a gifted, intelligent woman who not only played upon the themes of romanticism and alienation in her work, but lived them out to their ultimate conclusion in an act of self-denial and suppression when she killed herself in 1963. Did she lack what was needed to transcend her moments, months and years of romantic disillusion. Could she not see beyond her moments of sorrow? Her poetry and prose of the early 1960s reveal that she could not see her future as a creative thing. Life and circumstances seemed to be things that simply happened to her, not things she could bring about, change or improve. At times, rather than attempt to transcend her moments of despair, she engaged in imagining the fulfilment of her fears. It was perhaps at such a moment that Sylvia Plath put her head into a gas oven after barricading her sleeping children in a bedroom where she had placed mugs of milk and a plate of bread for them to find when they awoke.

When Plath met the man who would become her husband, she wrote of a "brilliant poet whose work I loved before I met him, a large, hulking, healthy Adam..." She described Ted Hughes to her mother as a "rugged, kind, magnificent man, who has no scrap of false vanity", whose mind was "magnificent, not hair-splitting or suavely politic".[11] After her marriage to Hughes in 1956, Plath was not so different from many of us who must attempt to reconcile domesticity and creativity. She was a "housewife" who wrote her poems early in the morning before her babies woke. When Ted Hughes left their home and marriage in 1962, Plath learned in the worst way that even a "hulking Adam" is a precarious foundation upon which to establish one's life and self. Resentment, self-loathing and envy were all Sylvia Plath could feel in the wake of Ted Hughes. She was the woman betrayed – not "fallen" – but the two are only opposite sides of the same coin. Both women, having invested their futures in men, carry the labels patriarchy doles out.

Sylvia Plath was endowed with creative gifts, but seemed unable to believe in her own qualities. In the 1950s and early 1960s there was little in the way of a feminist movement or feminist consciousness upon which Plath might have built a new interpretation and understanding of her personal history. Women's denial of their own qualities must be the concern of feminism today. The constant and dangerous denial of self in romance could threaten to drain any of us of our ability to appreciate and enjoy our own lives. We can become fixated, rigid and unable to see beyond the immediacy of this particular moment, this particular man, this particular need. Such fixation keeps us from envisioning independent futures of our own and stifles creative responses to living. The woman who says, "If I don't get this or that... If I can't keep this person or that person, I will die," is not creative in her thinking. Life assumes a tragic quality when we become obsessed with attaining ideal pleasures.

We must have dreams and wishes, but truly creative ideas are different from the illusion of idealised, romantic notions. Gloria Steinem emphasised this distinction: "Integrating a future self into the present is very different from the time-wasting, life-wasting habit of thinking about the future instead of the present; of indulging in magical thinking about what could happen; of living a deferred life."[12] There is another way of living —a way of greater ease — of living without illusion. If we do not require life to be without obstacles and do not expect ourselves to be all-knowing, then the difficult periods are just moments to transcend. Self-consciousness can point the way through broad transformations as awareness underlines potentials and opportunities for change, and it is "this trans — transmission, transpositions, transcendence — [that] is vitally necessary not only to our human life, but also to our creativity... [We] have to believe that there is a transcendental truth, that our life is not composed of simply a crisis or a trauma or a terrible moment which makes us feel that we might have to disappear or drop out or forget everything."[13]

The journey that I embarked upon – a path to independence and selfhood – is the same journey that many take. When Liam and I separated on our return to Ireland, I decided to move to "the middle of nowhere", literally making myself inaccessible to anyone. I rented a small beach bungalow, miles from any town. I think that somewhere within myself I still had sense enough to know that I needed to be alone with myself, to separate my problems and begin to sort them out. I didn't need my life to be as complicated as it had become and wished to scale it down in every way I could. In the process, I discovered and remembered things about myself that I had forgotten and lost track of. I remembered the music that I had always preferred to listen to before I gave over to someone else's preferences. I remembered the kinds of books I liked to read when I still had time to read. I didn't always sit with the television on as "background", as Liam and I had before. In formally "sharing" our son, sometimes I think we learned to divide our responsibilities to him for the first time.

I was now able to relish "my time" and made a point of doing the things I really liked. I started to jog and work out and take time in the preparation of my foods. I began to write and take myself seriously as a writer. I sat and listened to the utter silence of my home, took it in, and absorbed the calm so as to draw on it at other times. I watched the sorts of arts programs that Liam had never found interesting. I began to think about my future, now that I had one. I could have spent my time in loneliness, but instead was surprised to find ultimate faith in myself and belief in a future of some sort.

My newly-found independence and confidence also helped resolve my attachment to Evan. Not only did my attraction to him wane, but the misplaced reasons for which I had become attracted to him also became less relevant. I still thought about Evan sometimes, but I tried to resist romantic impulses, which had only confused me. I felt an incredible sense of accomplishment in succeeding every day, independently, in acquiring the most basic needs of my life – drinking water from a local well, heat from burning turf, simple food. I had my books and time to think, so I fixed one large room of my simple bungalow to be sitting-room, bedroom and study, all-in-one. That way I only needed to heat one room. Everything seemed self-contained, including myself.

It was not an accident that I was at least thirty miles away from anyone I knew, and because few people knew exactly where my bungalow was, I rarely had visits from anyone who was not local. I found myself happily alone in the heart of an isolated farming community. I walked to get my groceries, walked through gaps in the mountains, walked to the beach. Beyond that, I kept to my home, the yard and my writing, which was my only way of making a living. Everything seemed just barely enough, but exactly sufficient.

In *Goodbye Sleeping Beauty*, Madonna Kolbenschlag observes, "When aloneness is consciously chosen, it is creative as well as therapeutic. The first, and perhaps most important, effect of the choice is the cultivation of an inner life... Aloneness stirs us to explore and test our own personal resources. Ways of being, doing, making and enjoying that we might never suspect ourselves capable of suddenly flower in an enlarged existential space. Self-esteem is enhanced by survival and coping on one's own."[14]

Of course there were points when I still felt bewildered and empty. At such times, the support that I found in the work of conscious women seemed to come to me almost by accident – by watching films and reading books and magazines in the ordinary ways that we all do. I was not looking for, but found (and was ripe for understanding) feminist critiques. There were simple things – a videotape of a film about Anaïs Nin and Henry Miller, an old televised film by Lillian Hellman, a magazine article about Sylvia Plath, a talk-show interview with Gloria Steinem, the music and lyrics of Natalie Merchant. I was not a consciously-acting woman seeking out the materials with which to re-create herself. Coming to feminism was simply a matter of being – being here to receive information which is "out there" and reaching women, offering true moments of rescue, even in the most unlikely and isolated places.

The aspect of all this that was not accidental is that there are women conscientiously working to build the structures of feminism, each in her own way and from her own corner of the world. Their effects are being felt. Feminism is real. It is relevant. It is here and now. What was particularly important to me was the existence of a rich tradition of women's writing. The presence of feminism in media, particularly in the written word, is the primary vehicle for women's education about themselves and was the basis of my feeling a part of a feminist community. Even in the wilds of Donegal, I had access to books, broadcasts and telecasts that connected me and still connect me to a family of women who can help me understand and, this time, care for myself.

To find direction in my life I tried to sense and follow every clue that came my way. Friends, books, music, television, the natural world around me, letters, and notes I had written on my own reflections – all of this helped me understand who I am, what I like, what is most important to me, and some of the things I want and need to do with my life. This process does not happen in one day, or one year, and is never complete. But once I began to understand some of the things I really wanted and needed to do with my life, the fears and insecurities and all of those too real internal obstacles began to diminish.

Direction was not something anyone could give me, though many did help along the way. The transcending and dynamic dream, the visualisation of a future self, the wish which is truly creative and helps me progress was something that had to come from me. We all meet with difficult moments, crises that have dangerous, destructive potential. These need not be the end, but moments to become more aware of the lives before us.

It was during moments of despair that my wish was born. I began to write desperate notes which gradually became more lucid and, in essence, told me my real life as a woman was beginning. But still, I am not always so sure. Some days, thoughts and new understandings come easily to me. Other days, my child, my house and a pile of dirty dishes beckon. Then a day or two passes when I've accomplished nothing and I wonder if I will ever find anything within myself or in my writing again. I become angry at formless things and feel depressed – a disappointment to myself. Still, most of the time, I find a creative will to draw upon and do find that "imagination, which only teased me before, supports me now".[15]

It has taken other women's work and my own work to lead me out of despair and toward new ways of living. There was no material change in circumstances for me. I have never been well-off financially and I am still feeling the tremendous pressure of financial burdens that I cannot always meet. My troubles have not all dissolved and the world is not entirely rosy. During the difficult times, I find it helpful to consider the view that the "struggle itself is beautiful... You may be angry, you may be despairing, you may be depressed, but ultimately these are battles that can be won. And the battle for one's self-confidence and the battle to achieve an integrated image of yourself is a very wonderful one."[16]

As my own battles led me to seek creative solutions in self-expression, that expression has always led me back to my journey. For me, expression has been intimately tied to the conscious creation of my life as I have become more aware of and attentive to its details. The more energy I put toward my inner journey and into writing, the less I externalise interests and values in falsely gratifying activities like shopping, which used to give me a fleeting – and expensive – sense of satisfaction. I invest less of myself in primping, posing and being house-proud. The state of my body, arrangement of my hair, and order of my household are still important matters, but matters of fairly specific function and relevance, which no longer mirror my emotional state. When I do appreciate physical beauty in myself and in my home, it is a matter of aesthetics and not a misplaced measure of self-worth. It is not that the opinions or criticisms of others don't matter to me anymore. It is simply that they have finally taken their proper place in my life, somewhere behind my own views and estimates of myself.

With all of the changes I have found by looking within, I

have come to believe that the truly feminist iconoclast will be one who seeks sisterhood from bases of introspection and creative self-expression. The release and expression of my own creative impulses has saved me from the usual contradictions of women's lives – from the necessity of being loved by one man and attractive to many more, from being impelled toward housework while resenting the "duty" of it, from the urge to mother others while neglecting the nourishment of my own self, and from the desperate need for contact and seeming inability to experience it.

As women we have sought fulfilment in romance, marriage, motherhood, and now careers. Certainly all and any of these matters can enhance a life, but they cannot give meaning to life itself and any of them can end up being rather fragile investments. For too long we have misplaced our needs and for too long have been expected to be the listeners when others needed to express themselves. When women of the second wave of feminism attempted to be each other's confessors, they were criticised for focusing on problems, for adopting an ethos of "victimhood". Women of the third wave of feminism not only need to share their difficulties, but their solutions as well. We must take on the responsibility of finding our own creative ways to heal, expand and express our inner selves. When we have found these ways, we must do what we can to help other women find their voices as well.

The feminist community offers opportunities for us to give each other some of the nurturing and inspirational qualities we have been so accustomed to giving to men and children. But first there is work we can do ourselves, individually; then we will not merely add our problems to the collective burden of any group or movement. Every woman can work to begin separating and confronting her own defeats. By working on our own personal evolutions, we can discover the ideas which will add to the tremendous gifts feminism has already brought to women's lives. And we can do all of this while continuing to pose larger and broader challenges to the merely convenient arrangements and traditional structures of patriarchal society – because selfhood and sisterhood are not only compatible, but essential to each other.

Perhaps as more of us develop a natural fluency on "self", it may no longer seem in any way odd or unusual to speak with an emphasis on this most essential element of our existence. Over time, we might become so well-versed as to help men realise that the values of communication and expression and the language of emotions are not simply "womanly", but essentially human. We might begin to feel less dissonance between our internal and external worlds as we realise that we could live better with fewer pretenses, falsehoods and romanticisations. We might not need to spend so much of our energy merely coping as we find ourselves better able to realise our ability for more authentic and deeper experiences.

I don't know if any of this is possible, but I believe better relations and a better world are possible. I write of this future world, which I have never seen or felt. I imagine these meetings and friendships, of which I have only caught glimpses. But I do believe that the more articulate women become in the language of selfhood, the better we will be at expressing our genuine needs and interests to each other and to men.

Gloria Steinem emphasises: "If an analysis of sexism takes place only in relation to women, it adds to women's feeling of burden and fails to alert men to the ways in which they are being limited, too."[17] We know that men have felt uneasy about the evolution of women and have worried about becoming the "disposable" or dispensable sex. At times we may seem at cross-purposes with men, but most women do not see men as enemies, do not hate them, even if that is how things appear from a man's perspective. The situation is not that simple. We have all lived under the imposition of restrictive gender roles. In the process of our own transformations, we must become more sensitive to the fact that the dehumanising and de-personalising pressures of life also have affected men in profound ways. Men have been valued for what they have rather than who they are or what they feel. The other side of women's socialised dependence has been the pressure upon men to always be in control, not only of their emotions, but of all the practical matters of daily living.

When popular psychologist and author John Bradshaw analysed his inability to carry on coping with the image of being totally "together", of being the good provider and self-assured individual, his analysis led him to the same place where I have ended up: forced to consider "self" and its essential qualities. Bradshaw, with his theatrical manner, has become one of the most prominent advocates of "child within" therapy and has written books on the topic. Beyond the theatrics, the important point which Bradshaw helps to make is that the sham of constant and unwavering control is man's disease and the source of his own disorientation.

There was a time when I wanted to change my husband and believed that, if only he would change, my problems would be solved. I wondered if I could ever "rehabilitate" him, or if I would give up, leave and continue on my own destructive course from one wrong man to another. Undoubtedly, there were aspects of my husband and his behaviour that needed to change. What I have only recently realised is that Liam was just as unhappy with himself as I was with him, but he was afraid to admit to any weakness or crisis of self. In the meantime, I had completely deluded myself in imagining that I had the power to change another person. By the time my husband and I separated, I had become so disenchanted that I wholly believed the old cliché that "men don't change". What you see is what you get – live with it or leave, I thought.

Much of these thoughts were born of my feeling of cynicism and despair, and it was only when I stopped waiting for Liam to change and, finally, urgently, focused on myself that real progress began. It was only when I began to change that Liam saw the possibility of transformation and felt inspired and strengthened by witnessing it. He saw my moods level out – fewer outbursts, fits, depressions – and then began to believe that he might be able to change too, if he wanted to and if he worked on it. The important lesson we learned together is that men and women can inspire each other's liberation.

Liam is still in the midst of his own personal processes and whether or not he accomplishes the things he wants will be up to him. I can identify with him. I can recognise something like my own humanity in him. Having abandoned our old scripts, we "no longer live in spurious peace by avoiding each other."[18]

Liam has already transcended his old self more than I imagined anyone could. He has found acceptance of self in the fact that not all things are within his control, so that for the first time he can really appreciate the things he is certain of. And because he no longer clings to the pretence that everything is under his control, he keeps fewer secrets and is not afraid to let me so close that I will find them out. He finds the sort of deep confidence in his true self that his false pretenses never could have brought him. If there is a "new man" – or will be a man of the future – he will be a man who is not made whole by pretenses and façades, but by engaging in the emotion and art of human relationship.

In our marriage as it used to be, we would never have been able to communicate at the deepest levels. We had talked about our futures and things that we wanted to accomplish, but in all of those discussions we were still living out the roles which we felt were expected of us. There were many important conversations that were not happening. If crises had not brought confession, we might never have confided that we were not sure of where we were going or what we wanted. We had lost track of our own feelings and interests and, as we became increasingly detached, fighting became the substitute for communication. Arguing had been one of the few ways that I felt able to assert my views and express my resentment. And since fighting has always been one of the few ways in which men have been able to express any emotion at all, it became our only common language.

When Liam and I were at our lowest points, I had no interest in preserving our relationship, but needed to preserve myself. Surprisingly, I found that the lessons I learned for my survival were the same that could save my relationship. I was surprised by this because, so many times, I had felt my self and our relationship were at odds. But just as I had to begin to view the low points of my life as valleys that could be over-come and traversed, I began to see that the low points of my marriage might also be transcended. As I felt myself change and was beginning to see that Liam could change when he wanted to, I realised that relationships can change. We will not always be caught in the desperate moments – neither as indi-viduals, nor as a couple. My marriage was terrible and felt terrible, but it was not condemned to be an awful marriage forever.

A realistic approach to relationships would include the idea that not every problem will be worked out by "communica-tion". On the contrary, the difficult periods tend to be so long and arduous that even the most basic forms of communication break down and degenerate. Many men will not even know when their wives are unhappy, nor will they understand the seriousness and extent of this unhappiness. In many ways, marriage is just another opportunity and context in which we find out about ourselves through our experience with others. When two people enter into a committed relationship, they enter into an agreement to carry on their personal journeys near to each other. But, ultimately, the creative effort that we exert is something that will tell us more about ourselves than our mates.

Before a marriage can work, men and women must realise that whatever we are is there, inside of us, and within our own powers. Events and people can bring certain qualities out, but that is all. We have no hope of changing each other, only broadening ourselves. Once my husband and I realised that, our lives improved. It's not that everything is perfect now, but things are less dangerously unbalanced. There is less seething resentment, less melodrama and less romantic distortion. We still have arguments, but now there are fewer subtexts. There is less potential for all of the little, petty arguments to become larger, symbolic conflicts. (In my case, even a humble wall-hanging could take on enormous proportions.) We have cleared the air. Our life together is no longer charged with the deep anxieties which kill love.

We communicate about our needs more effectively now, understanding exactly what is at risk if we do not. Each of us understands that the other has limits and priorities, and we try not to make unreasonable demands on each other. My husband understands how important it is for both of us to enjoy self-expressive lives, and that we will both have to adjust our plans and schedules in order to make these things possible for each other. Each of us expects the other to have a life, first, and then a relationship. Each of us wants these things for the other and is willing to make adjustments and negotiate responsibilities.

We do not have a perfect marriage, because we do not possess perfect selves. But we are committed to our own progress and growth, and to helping each other realise our potential. Though our lives are not without difficulties, often I do feel that these are the days of true expansion. All of the rest, including the blunders, might have been preparation for this time. Before, we were sleepwalking. It is only the understanding of our own subconscious insecurities that has explained the patterns we have lived and has freed us from carrying on in self-destructive modes.

It seems ironic that human beings seek knowledge of the future but fear their own unconscious worlds. We have invested tremendous amounts of money and time in everything from daily newspaper horoscopes and astrological chat lines, to readings of palms and tea-leaves. But it is knowledge of the *past* and my own self that has freed me. Perhaps we would have much less fear of the future and see much less mystery in it if we understood the templates which guide our lives.

My husband and I have even begun to view our relationship as having a sort of existence and unconscious past of its own. Sensitivity to this past frees us from making the mistakes we made before. Knowledge of our individual insecurities and past wounds, coupled with an awareness of what we have already been through together, keeps our relationship from being fraught with a fear of our future together.

Where I feel pride, it is in having made it through a difficult experience and in no longer being as naïve as I once was. My husband and I are together now, though it has not been easy. Despite all of the uncertainty I have felt in this, I believe in myself now as I never have before. Basically, I like myself and I feel that I will be all right. I think this would be the case whether or not my husband and I had reunited, and I know this must be the case, whether or not we stay together.

Many people might wonder how we cope with the knowledge of infidelity and the erosion of trust that comes with that. While infidelity signals an end to many marriages, we have found ways to accept our difficulties as devastating storms that tore through our marriage, leaving our love still standing. Part of the reason we stay together is because we believe that we did not go into our marriage intending to hurt each other. I can only imagine that we found ourselves in the situations we were in by circumstance, neglect, and an unanswerable neediness. So we blame the circumstances, particularly the unconscious circumstances, and set out to unravel them and change our situations.

Sometimes friends are specifically curious about how we cope in our sexual relations with each other, knowing that each has been with others while we had once sworn monogamy to each other. First of all, we had to realise that the true sources of our infidelities did not have much to do with sex. Sex was the expression, and that fact does hurt sometimes. The human mind can paint some terrible pictures. Each of us does sometimes have flashes of imagination which depict an infidelity, and recall the threat and pain it involved. What we may have thought were peak moments have become gradually diminishing nightmares, however, with the main memory being that feeling of deception.

In many cases like our own, sex is the distraction from problems that are actually much more complex, though transformable. But people who get through this sort of thing and still love each other don't simply forget. We have let go of some recollections and can let flashes of imagination pass and fade because we want to hold on to something that we have together which is more solid now because of the difficulties we have gone through and lessons we have learned. We let go and give over the petty hurts and lingering insecurities in order to hold on to the more vital aspects of our lives.

For us, maturity in our relationship has come with shedding what we are not, and then balancing what we are in relation to each other. We have found ways to stop punishing each other as we increase faith in our own individual, unique selves.

We realise that we still want to make our journeys together. The fact that we still want to be together is important enough that we hold on to each other and let other things go. It isn't always easy and it isn't painless, but it may be worth it.

Some people ask if we have been able to re-learn trust. We have not. To recall some of the events that have happened is to touch a wound and call up the insecurities we once lived all day and all night. We are no longer innocents, yet I feel as though I am the most constant wife, the wife of greatest fidelity – not innocent faith, but something else. Certainly it is true that we have lost simple, young faith, which is a beautiful but fragile thing. What we have instead is the knowledge that the love between us has a sufficiently deep source to be a creative force at our weakest moments. It inspires us to begin seeking healing solutions even when our relationship is most fragmented. This gives me a different kind of faith and comfort now. We have traded in naïve trust and innocent faith for a love that has been tested and seasoned with experience.

Madonna Kolbenschlag suggests that "love depends on a high degree of self-confidence and self-sufficiency, and at the same time on a recognition of the uncertainty and contingency of a relationship that ultimately transcends one's own control and will. This gives the creative relationship a dynamic and dialectical quality; conviction and doubt marry each other."[19] The bad times can become stages that you are almost grateful for when you begin to appreciate these times as periods of challenge and personal growth. The moments of reconciliation can be moments of a kind of grace and new beginning.

It would have been perfect to have reached this point

through nothing but clear thinking and balanced actions. But in reality "it is always something we look on as evil in ourselves that forces us toward wholeness. It is a threat, a fly-in-the-ointment, something that upsets our ego worlds and our production-line lives… a neurosis that suddenly wells up and disrupts our lives, forcing us to look for the meaning behind what we can't explain."[20]

Mothers of Invention

✦

MY MARRIAGE AND motherhood are among the
major activities and interests of my life today, but
they are part of a larger, creative life with its own
rhythm, its own peaks and ebbs. So when a friend of mine
claimed a severe case of writer's block lasting six years, it was
easy for me to relate to her problem and to console her, saying
that I had had more false starts than I could remember and
had failed to finish anything of any significance for four years.
She responded, "But that's understandable. You've had children. At least you have something to show for four years. I
haven't even got a baby to show for my years. There's no
excuse for me."

I must say that my sons are often tremendous consolation
for me, but never seemed sufficient excuse for my failure to
produce my own creative work. While they themselves have

been a lot of work and will be a lot more, I don't feel I can ever list them among my credentials. There have to be ways for women to create and find meaning, beyond relationships and child-rearing. I recognise that motherwork and house-work tend to block expressive work insofar as they do not allow much time for creativity nor provide the atmosphere for cultivating an interior life. But we must find ways to order the multiple aspects and roles of our lives, so as not to have to choose between them, for the choice is usually at the expense of our self-expression and we know that is not a price we can afford to pay any longer.

There was a space of eight years between the second and third of Adrienne Rich's books. Hers was not simply a bad case of writer's block. During the eight intervening years she was raising three sons and was "writing very little, partly from fatigue... partly from the discontinuity of female life with its attention to small chores, errands, work that others constantly undo, small children's constant needs."[1] When she did write, it was often at the kitchen table, her work squeezed into meagre spaces of time, after the feedings and before the baths, between cycles of the laundry. Such configurations of house-work and motherwork determined the form of Rich's work. She felt that "poetry, as much as journals and letters and diaries, has been an almost natural women's form ... for the kinds of reasons that I wrote very short poems in the fifties – because I had to write while the children were napping, between chores".[2]

While Rich was busy raising her sons during the 1940s and 1950s, Western society was undergoing an upsurge in the "emotionalization of housework", as part of the ideological effort to encourage women to return to their homes and vacate jobs for World War II veterans. But attempts to endow household tasks with the emotional charge of "wifely and motherly love" have only put gilt upon the real strains and monotony of domestic work. Investing these tasks with the status of a domestic "science" has done little to benefit anyone except the manufacturers of cleansing products. The reality of domestic labour is that housework is still physically taxing, and can feel isolating if it is not shared and fairly divided. There is no way to reason that any sort of work which is constantly being undone, and always needs to be redone, can feel spiritually uplifting. Despite labour-saving devices, cleansing aids and the conveniences of the modern kitchen, at the end of the day, housewives still speak of feeling frustrated, bored and left empty by their work. What Edith Stein wrote in 1949 still holds: housewifery continues to have the same mind-numbing effect, and still means "hopping from one unrelated, unfinished task to another... nothing leads quite logically from one thing to another."[3]

Most of us feel a deep contempt for the view of woman as half-servant. But the fact that I have, at the same time, lived this role has not only brought confusion, but also an understanding of a range of insights that many feminists have denied. In *The Second Stage,* Betty Friedan went a long way towards recognising that the individualism of mainstream, workplace feminism has not only been irrelevant to many women, but has tended to exclude them. Katie Roiphe's view that feminism should be about "being successful and powerful" represents the sort of narrow, careerist feminism that has alienated many of the house-bound wives and mothers who

– isolated and unorganised – may need feminism more urgently than most. Friedan emphasised that we are more likely to connect, across classes and races, under the strain of the wife and mother roles than through any other associations, experiences, or networks. Unfortunately, in response to these remarks, some radicals mistakenly accused Friedan of "reviving" the notion of woman-as-compassionate-mother, as though she had invented it.

Bridging the gaps in analyses which have distanced motherhood from feminism, and overcoming patriarchal associations with "mother", will take some work. Mother has had a bad run over the last hundred years or so, beginning with Freud. Having been blamed for just about every fault of traditional socialisation, even radical feminists have confused the object of patriarchy for the representative of it. Motherhood is a choice – and it should always be a choice – but since it is a choice most of us will make, a bit of understanding and compassion would go a long way in avoiding the alienation of a vast pool of potential feminists. It has been more than wrong to require the rejection of mother in the definition of one's feminism; it has been nonsensical, ironic, sometimes impossible.

A short while ago I read a young journalist's reflections about her feminism in *The Irish Times*. Her view is representative of a fairly common expression of feminism that alienates and offends many women: "The majority of us remain motivated by the desire to build a life as unlike our mothers' lives as possible. I resisted the desire to leave school at the age of 15 and conceive my first child a year later. I am 27, but I work outside the home and do not have four children under

the age of nine. In these and many other ways I have chosen
... a life unlike my mother's."[4]

It is ironic that, in the process of articulating her own feminism, this feminist patronises another woman. She writes of
women of the previous generation as though they simply had
poor judgements and "desires". She suggests that her mother
lacked sufficient discipline to resist leaving school and sufficient restraint to resist conceiving. I think we have to mature
in our feminism enough to understand that our mothers, and
all mothers, have experienced the same patriarchy that we
perceive and rail against. If our mothers have not been politicised, we have to hope that we can create more opportunities
for developing feminism in our generation, and the next
generation of mothers. The journalist I have quoted may be a
good, sincere, insightful feminist, but is still lamenting that it
was Katie Roiphe's mother who "probably could have quoted
everything Kate Millet ever wrote" while her own could only
supply information on "dealing with German measles and
weaning".[5]

Madonna Kolbenschlag has commented upon the "familiar
protests" of daughters who are "not like" their mothers: "'Oh,
no, I'm not at all like my mother. It was my father – my grand-
mother – who influenced me most.' Denials, inevitably contra-
dicted by the reality. Daughters invariably absorbing, repeating
a mother's emotional life. Self-knowledge comes much too
late."[6]

After spending most of her life trying to distance herself
from her mother's fate, Gloria Steinem came up with the right
question: "Are there generations of daughters, each one
rebelling against the false image forced on the generation

before, never knowing that we would have loved and admired our mothers all the more if they had been able to blossom as their true selves?"[7]

Adrienne Rich suggests that "the cathexis between mother and daughter – essential, distorted, misused – is the great unwritten story" and is a relationship which has been "minimised and trivialised in the annals of patriarchy."[8]

My mother and your mother are not merely the images in which they have been moulded and socialised. Of course, traditional notions of parenting as the exclusive domain of "mother" do need to be rejected, but instead of rejecting the women who happened to be our mothers, we can learn so much more by separating them from their fates long enough to try to understand and identify with their predicaments. It is patriarchal society, not mother herself, which equates parenting with mothering and has not only tried to make the terms synonymous, but has also endowed "mother" with almost mystical "feminine" qualities.

In reality, as Anne Lamott attests in *Operating Instructions: A Journal of My Son's First Year*, much of mothering comes as a shock – a mixture of wonder, joy, exhaustion, despair and plain hard work. That is what parenting is like. With each child, both mothers and fathers find themselves getting to know a brand new acquaintance, except that this one might be the most demanding, dependent, impatient person you have ever met. And this little person does not go away. Once I became a mother, I could never believe the suggestion that parenting comes "naturally" to anyone. Everything I do feels like a struggle and a learning experience. To go through this and, at the same time, feel unable to identify with the important and sometimes life-saving elements of feminism, is to feel very alone indeed.

Recognising the strains and contradictions contained in the lives and roles of women is what feminism really should be about. The most radical feminist consciousness must include the notion that sisterhood also exists among potential feminists – women who have not had the time and space to develop their selves. In acknowledging the roles of mothers and wives, Friedan was not trying to reinforce tradition, but was considering the multiplicity of lives women lead. It was only while failing to face these complexities that the development and perpetuation of the all-things-to-all-people, all-juggling "supermom" freak show could have occurred. This combination of paid and unpaid work was sold to us as "liberation", but was more amusing to conservatives than anyone else. It has brought more in the way of a privileged-class contracting-out of parenting duties to poor women than any real challenge to gender roles. Emigrant women, in particular, could and do speak volumes on this topic, as they are often hired to do "motherwork" for others.

Just down the road from me, in Derry – where men have been unemployed for generations and women have always been the preferred, docile workers in the shirt factories – mothers could have told us that paid work, in and of itself, would not bring liberation. It may bring some redistribution of authority within families, but no real changes in the assumption of gender roles. Derry mothers knew the strain of the "double day", combining paid work in the factory with unpaid work at home, long before American social scientists gave their malady a name. Plenty of working-class American women knew it too. Derry is only an example of the class reality which middle-class feminists have tended to overlook.

There is so much that we could have learned. There is so much that we have only denied and misunderstood by seeming to define feminism in opposition to the domesticity that most women have never really been able to escape. For as long as feminism has seemed to require rejection of mother or exclusion of motherhood, it has asked too much of many women and has denied vital aspects of our own character. What we need is a feminism which contains a truly independent definition of womanhood, never defined merely in opposition to some other generation, lifestyle or gender.

While we develop a truly independent feminism of the self through a third wave, this time we should appreciate the fact that in motherhood women share an experience that crosses all of our other affiliations. Here we have one of the few experiences that binds us across nations, ethnicities, races and classes. (In Northern Ireland, where I gave birth to my children, the maternity ward is one of the few places where Catholic and Protestant women meet.)

We cannot afford to disregard the fact that motherhood is a connection that has a tremendous politicising potential, as it slaps us in the face with all sorts of gender inequities that we, as young women and young feminists, never had been in a position to confront before. Perhaps here, in being wives and mothers, we face the most insidious and most rigidly assumed aspects of patriarchy. These bastions remain, even when the more obvious structural and legal barriers have been dismantled. When the wives and mothers who will help to define the future of feminism feel that they are losing their footing, they should feel supported by their sisters; they are, after all, moving closer to eliminating the foundations of patriarchy.

The days when the pillars shook in my own home were not easy or happy days, but they have led to better times. On many of my worst days, all of my small frustrations with the details of our household became larger and larger until they seemed to dominate all of life. I have always hated housework and I hate cooking meals, except on the rare occasion when I decide to cook something special. Most of the time, I loathe this work. I resent it before I even begin. Yet, up until a short while ago, I was quite diligent in domestic chores – doing laundry, ironing, grocery shopping, dusting and vacuuming twice weekly, with daily dish-washing and weekly planning of meals. We had a lovely household and it ran like a charm. My husband and son would never have had to search for a clean pair of socks and we were never embarrassed if visitors arrived unexpectedly.

But there came a time when, I suppose, I "cracked". I had gone a bit loopy over housework many other times. I had roared at people who left rooms in a mess. I chastised my husband for leaving empty wrappers and old newspapers around, as though he knew or expected that someone else was around to clean up after him. That was not my job, I made it clear, so he should not walk the earth imagining that some-one was right behind him, tidying. Eventually, I really lost my ability to cope with the futile monotony of my domesticity. Housework was always looming, never finished. (Working outside of the home had never helped me to escape it; most of it was still to be done when we would all get home in the evenings, and most of it still fell to me.) One day I seemed to "wake-up" to find myself crying in my spotless kitchen and, despite all of my labour hours, feeling I had done nothing for months or years. I was empty, bored, sickened, fed-up. The way I saw things, even the paid work I did was really for someone else's glory and benefit – it was only the fact that it was paid that made it gratifying at all. Even at that, the money it brought in went back into running that oppressive household of mine. Rarely did I feel there was money left to spend on "extras", like fun and recreation.

Just then, with my head down on the kitchen table, I heard the telephone ring. I probably would have told whoever it happened to be at the other end that I hated my life. The caller happened to be my mother-in-law. Desperate to confess to someone, I told her: "At the end of each morning, I have a lovely, clean kitchen, but that is all I have. And no sooner have I tidied it than it is messed again. I have nothing to show for my mornings, my afternoons, my months and years. Every day, it is the same." The monotonous tone of my household routine seemed to have become the tone of my whole life. I hardly had to explain this to my mother-in-law. As though she recognised a terrible familiarity, she asked if the kitchen was not a diversion and distraction from other issues. Why had the kitchen begun to represent everything I resented, but felt obliged to do?

Once it was put to me plainly, it did not take me long to realise my need to express other aspects of myself. I decided to commit more of myself and my time to finding ways to do that. But – it was undeniable – there still seemed something very real about the urgency and necessity of housework. Before I could begin any more creative occupation, my kitchen had to be in order, with dirty dishes washed, dried and stacked in the cupboard. There was this preliminary ritual to my writing, in which I was almost pathologically driven to attend to the dishes first. And so I would begin by simulating a kind of order amongst bits of stoneware, flatware, pottery and glass.

For the first few weeks of a new schedule, with a new emphasis upon writing as the priority for all of my empty spaces of time (many of which had to be created and negotiated with the help of others), I had to wrench myself out of my former routine, to set aside a time for disciplined reflection and personal meditation. It was only when I enforced this restructuring of my time and priorities that I realised the pull of housework, which had simply become a part of myself. I still do not fully understand the power the house had over me. I don't know if I will ever understand the reasons why I took on so many petty tasks and felt guilty when I did not. In fact, I think there might not be any good reasons at all, only ritual, so now I find other ways to express my devotions.

I had to separate housework from its emotional charge. Many mornings it took a huge amount of discipline to keep myself focused on my own authentic needs, and away from domestic tasks. In the process of making self-expression a priority, I often found myself having to justify the deferment of housework. I was learning that it would take at least as much re-socialisation to resist my "duties" as was required to begin this life of routinised housework in the first place. I had to retrain myself to resist the beckoning of dishes.

Perhaps it is interesting that it was only when I began to slack off from housework that I realised I was the only one in the house for whom it held emotional connotations. I found out that I was the only one who had really cared very much whether the dishes were done in the morning, or evening, or left to lie for a day or two. And, while dish-washing was an aspect of the "science" of our home that I felt uniquely qualified for, I was relieved to find that there was no harm done if I left dirty dishes to the genius of someone else's hands. Increasingly I found myself like Judy Chicago, who wrote of her own struggle as a woman artist, realising the extent to which the pattern that I thought my husband and son had instilled was of my own making: "All of that so-called tight duty, tight pattern... was self-imposed."[9]

The good news is that the pressure we have felt is just air, once we decide to view it that way. The restructuring of time and interests can be done, and no one suffers. In fact, everyone benefits from the improvement of my mood as I approach a greater sense of fulfilment and purpose. I no longer see housework as an expression of my caring or concern, and find myself more generous and creative in other expressions of my love for the people near to me. Any misplaced resentment I harboured has diminished and no longer clouds our relationships. Even mundane tasks are less oppressive when housework is in its proper perspective, as something that often needs be done, but will wait for a convenient time. We have minimised our housekeeping, yet everything still seems to get done, perhaps not as often as before. We have made more time for enjoying our lives together. What tasks remain, we negotiate as much as we can.

Housework is still necessary, but we recognise that it is only important for aesthetic, not emotional, reasons. When I am content in a creative aspect of my life, then tasks around the house become more reasonable parts of a larger pattern and larger aesthetic of life. Our home has gone back to being what it was intended to be – not a place of oppression, but one of warmth and shelter. Now, whatever energy I give the house, the house gives back to me in comfort. It helps to provide an atmosphere which encourages imagination and growth. I only needed to unleash my own creative urges to put this house in its proper place, as a backdrop to an active and varied life.

I know it can be difficult for any woman to place her own needs before those of others or even before those of a house. Even when we have managed to take those first few steps toward accomplishing our own creative work, it is still difficult to concentrate and to push through each transition in the successive phases of creation. My own work and powers of concentration had been so overshadowed by the distractions of domestic tasks that I thought distraction itself was uniquely a problem of women artists.

I had imagined that men would have no similar divisions of obligations, no equivalent strain in their productive and creative discipline; and that women, unless able to put their own needs above all others, would never be equal in the world of truly focused artists. So it helped me to hear comedian and novelist Ben Elton admit that he is constantly drawn to larger and larger mugs of tea between pages, then paragraphs, and lines. This comment may seem trivial, but it made me realise that women and men both fight distraction. It comforts me, because women have needed to feel equal, even in this way. If we can understand that men have also had to fight distraction, then we can feel ourselves on more equal footing. And given that dedication is hardly a quality foreign to us, we can really believe in women's full participation in worlds of creation, once we divest ourselves of our diffuse devotions and reclaim the interests that have been diverted.

Critically examining my housework and motherwork, and finding reasonable ways to deal with my many obligations, were principal aspects of realising ways to live for myself. Incorporating my diverse roles into a lifestyle which gave me time and space for self-expression was the leap I had to take when I began taking myself seriously as a whole, varied, woman. It took an effort to work against my conditioning and to find ways of making the structures of my life more flexible. We need more models, more creative ideas about reconciling the traditional opposition between domesticity and our own interests, more discussion of the ways in which our daily schedules as wives and mothers combine, or fail to combine, with our desire to lead more diverse lives. In the next few pages I describe some of the efforts I made, and suggest ways to begin identifying and prioritizing your own needs.

In *Revolution From Within* Gloria Steinem offers some simple exercises by which any of us can begin tapping into our subconscious selves. She asks readers to write about what they felt they lacked in their childhoods and, later, asks them to describe their "ideal lover". She earnestly asks readers to begin discovering their needs for themselves – creating the qualities of the ideal lover in themselves, providing themselves with the missing aspects of a lost childhood.

I must admit that when I first tried Steinem's exercises, I laughed them off. I would not take them seriously. Then, in my nervousness, I realised that there were many other "simple" questions about myself which made me extremely uncomfortable. Gradually, as answers evolved over months of reflection, I realised that I had been lacking the most basic degree of internal focus. And I realised that these exercises, even if they did seem banal at first, led to more complicated processes within myself.

The point of answering basic questions about ourselves is to encourage us to spend some time thinking about, and in many cases remembering, the essential elements of our true selves. Remembering the things that we like, the tastes we prefer, the prospects that appeal to us – all of this provides a basis to work from when we are seeking the nature of our authentic needs and true direction in life. If it helps you to think back to some time when you lived your life as fully and independently as you can ever imagine, then do so and recollect your interests at that time. If you feel that you never experienced a really independent, self-sufficient or self-contained time in your life, imagine what it would be like if you did. Don't fall back upon romantic illusions of living through the perfect man, or winning the lottery, or any context which suggests having your needs "taken care of". Instead imagine what it would be like in a situation in which you took care of your own needs. How would you be living then? What kind of music would you listen to? What sorts of friends would you have? What would you be doing in your free time? All of your answers should be the sort that please you, not simply the answers that will please or impress other people.

Maybe it is significant that I found myself answering such questions most honestly when I was feeling distressed at the life that I was leading. The rest of the time I might have managed to adjust and cope, just enough to carry on lying to myself. But when I wanted to chuck it all, I found myself full of the kind of angry, revolutionary energy that brings new ideas. Dostoevsky suggested that authentic spiritual experiences are most likely to happen when we find ourselves at the end of our ropes, that "One has to be a bit ill to really feel alive."[10] Perhaps I was taking part in a feminist tradition, drawing upon the same sort of personal anger from which feminism sprang, placing my anger in a context that defined it, politicised it and brought consciousness to me in the same way that feminism has brought new perspectives to politics.

In your own tumult, focus on simple self-orienting exercises. Even in moments of "madness", let these exercises suggest new sensitivities and a new vision of yourself. Over time, you will find yourself constructing your own ways to transcend the predicaments of the moment, and then taking the small steps that can change the whole tone of your life. In other words, you will be moving toward a new consciousness.

Another tried and tested technique I have used to understand what really matters to me is by making "top ten" lists. Make a top ten list of the music you would want to have, if you could only have ten albums for all time. Then go back to listening to that music. Make a top ten list of books you would want to keep, if you could only keep ten. Resist any temptation to be simply practical in your choices. Do not think in terms of the usefulness of keeping an encyclopedia because of its breadth, but in terms of the essential qualities of a book of poetry because of its depth. Value soulful needs over practical uses. You could make a list of ten things you have wanted to do and take action toward doing them. Make a list of the top ten possessions you would want to take with you if you had to move to a new country and could only take a certain amount with you. You might be surprised at how easy it is to say good-bye to things – like shedding several unnecessary skins.

You can work on top ten lists on lots of things that matter to you, but in order for these lists to suggest directions for your life, there is one strict guideline to observe: avoid anything that suggests having your needs taken care of through romance or luck. You will be setting yourself up for disappointments and doing little to secure true direction for yourself unless these lists are within realistic realms and suggest things you can start to recreate or approach anew in your life.

When I was trying to remember who Peg was and what she liked, the first change I decided on was to go back to using my maiden name more often. It sounds a trivial matter, perhaps, but, for me, it was symbolic of an aspect of myself which I needed. My maiden name was the label that had identified me during those times when I centred on developing and educating myself. Simply hearing that label again, and responding to it, did adjust my perspective slightly and was one concrete verification of a somewhat separate identity, distinct from the associations I had gained through marriage and motherhood. The point was not to exclude my husband, but to include myself again – a symbolic correction of my private complicity with male-centred and male-defined relationships.

The second thing I did was attempt to re-create the essence of the times in my life when I was independent and centred on my own development. Part of recreating the essence of independent life was in pulling out my old albums and tapes.

I began listening to Steely Dan again. Hearing their tunes in the air went a long way toward re-creating an atmosphere of self-seeking, critical thinking, and reminded me of the pure joy of the "free" time I had spent up on my roof in Berkeley. I remembered long, warm afternoons when I would lie there, in the warmth of the evening sun, listening to my music, reading my books, and feeling kind of high the scent of the jasmine bushes below.

I also started reading the sorts of books I had liked when I still did the choosing and purchasing, and decided to start making time to read more. I had never been much interested in fiction, though fiction is all we had bought for years. I remembered, or finally paid attention to, the fact that from a very early age I was not even interested in fairy tales. Even as a young girl, I really had always preferred the angles of auto-biographical writing, from *The Diary of Anne Frank* to *Black Like Me*. So I went back to reading autobiographies of all sorts. The fact that I was profoundly interested in the auto-biographies of both well-known and lesser-known people, historical figures and contemporary ones, led me to realise that there was something in the autobiographical exercise itself that interested me. It was the opportunities presented by self writing about self that I found exciting – autobiography, very much separate and distinct from biography. I followed every clue back to my original interests. Increasingly, I found myself making connections between my former, independent self and my present self. I realised that there were continuities, however vague, and that there was an essence to me which survived and transcended. That very fact helped me begin to believe in the possibility of a future self as well.

Gradually, I began to remember who I was and what I liked. I began to understand what it meant to "just be yourself", beyond the cliché. The answers to questions about myself began to come more easily and I felt more strongly about them than I ever remembered feeling before. Soon I realised that I was not having to delve back in time to recall aspects of myself, but that I had rejuvenated and breathed life back into strong and certain aspects of me: the choices, thoughts, preferences, interests, likes and dislikes which help to describe a person. I spoke in a voice that was no longer muffled, embarrassed, apologetic or drowned out by the opinions of others. It seemed like I was remembering what life was supposed to feel like.

Consciousness and Creation

I N WRITING THIS book I have begun to understand why
so many feminist books tend to be collections of essays –
fragments snatched and ideas culled from the experiences
of busy, over-extended women, called contributors. I could
end this in the way that many of these sorts of feminist books
do, with notes on our wishes for the future and our hopes for
the next generation. I would like to give a final nod, but the
pieces written here are different from the usual compilations.
In writing this I have felt that I am putting together the pieces
of a puzzle, and the puzzle is me. I can't pretend to know the
conclusion, but I know that it will be found by exploiting the
potential of the self, and the contribution which the creativity of the self can make to both feminism and our broader
culture.

In this book I have attempted to progress our intellectual

examination as feminists, finally looking critically enough at the many traps around us and then deeply enough within ourselves to realise that many of those snares have been sustained by our own romanticisations, illusions and compliance. Yet even at this time – when "self" has become a fad industry with a myriad of therapies – the major criticism of a personal feminism has been that it focuses too much on internal processes and distracts feminists from formulating political agendas and programmes of action. Raising women's consciousness is not thought to be much good for getting things done! But in my own feminist evolution, I found that I needed to start with my self, then expand to my personal relationships, and then expand my consciousness further to embrace wider national and global concerns. This process starts slowly, but gains a tremendous momentum. An acute and sincere awareness of one's own humanity makes it easier to recognise – and difficult to deny – the humanity of others. And it is when the value of humanity is recognised at the very core and essence of one's own existence that an active defence of its integrity on a wider scale may become most urgent and sincere.

For the moment, we are caught in a phase that sometimes seems impossible to transcend, where societies recognise and value the self primarily in terms of production and consumption. All around us we can see the crime, the corruption of governments, the perversion and duplicity of their agents, and an increasing apathy among individuals who have witnessed more than they can understand. Politics and sociology have not been able to respond to the depths of our needs. Psychology is frequently diminished to analysing the mechanisms by which we manage to function, but not really live; philosophy is marginalised, relegated to an aspect of history, an anachronism, a relic. Our failure to link the importance of self-development to social integrity and political morality, and the taboos against introspection and subjectivity which we have internalised, diminish the quality of human life every day. We do not express – we are too busy just coping. Many of us are also beyond coping and have come to rely upon anaesthetics of various sorts, in epidemic proportions.

Feminism has been mistaken and narrow in thinking that women would find fulfilment in the workplace and that politics alone could address the range of our crises. We have failed to analyse our compulsion toward the romantic illusions which parody our own unfulfilled expressive and emotional needs. Having sought our fulfilment in romance, marriage, motherhood and careers, we have only now begun to understand Gloria Steinem's view that happiness, satisfaction and self-confidence are "most likely to come from intrinsic interest, not external reward, from a desire to express the true self."[1]

Self-awareness, with its creative implications, commands all of the powers of the mind and brings them to our assistance when we need them most. We possess the capacity to re-create ourselves when we feel destroyed. This creative capacity is what I found and depended upon in my worst moments and this is the realm that has been the concern of the most personal strands of feminism.

It is expansive for women to recognise the existence of inner selves which have been denied and repressed. It is revolutionary to feel a sense of intrinsic worth and recognise the worth of other selves. And it is exciting to open lines of communication, despite insecure moments when we still are not sure that there is anything inside.

I recently clicked on a television programme about the wives of professional athletes in which one of the women was asked about her worries, needs, interests. "None really," she said. She only worried for her family and hoped that the future would be all right for the children, that her husband would avoid injury and that his job would remain secure. All of these matters are totally reasonable concerns, of course. The reporter pressed on and asked what her concerns were for herself. "None. Nothing in particular." Hobbies? "Going to the matches." Personal interests? "None in particular." The man conducting the interview obviously could not quite understand. He kept trying for a response, without realising that she had already given every response she knew how to give, and that she spoke volumes to any woman who recognised her situation.

Maybe you are not so far from the situation I have just described. It was not so long ago for me either. Certainly I recognise aspects of this "nothingness" in women who are close to me, who are educated, intelligent, competent and talented. And I have my own weak and insecure moments when I feel uncertain of the depth of my source. Sometimes it is a shock to realise that we have not really come as far as we like to think, that there is so much work still to do, and that much of the progress we have seen has not been at the deepest and most significant levels. Caitlin, wife of Dylan Thomas, claimed to resort to affairs in order to give herself "the illusion of something going on" in her own life. She considered herself "the biggest misfit of the age." She was an accomplished poet, but she could feel no faith in her work beside the genius of her husband.

For a long while in my own life, the work of the men around me always seemed more important than my own. I subscribed to the notion that the only way I could be great as a woman would be by being great for a great man – to foster his self and nurture his creativity. I imagined that this would be the way to an exciting and bohemian life. I did not see how conventional my life was and how I had bought into one of the most traditional images of womanhood, that of the muse: the one who nurtures the artist, makes the world a more tolerable place for him, inspires his work. While many of us have fallen into this role, it has always been misguided to imagine that men could produce, and unfair to ask them to produce, the work that would express our own selves.

It is ironic that, even as the woman-muse generates spirit and passion in the lives of those she touches, she rarely experiences that creative force with any more personal intensity. So the image of the muse brings up important questions about womanhood and the nature of creativity, and brings the connectedness of issues of feminism and self-expression into bold relief. The very notion of the muse is peculiar in suggesting that the artist is not directly responsible for creation – that inspiration is not something the artist possesses, but a mystical, mysterious and external agent. Separating the artist from the creative impulse is not helpful to any of us. Less helpful again is the association of the muse with womanhood – a new pedestal of sorts, but just another idealised position which never offers full satisfaction or full possession of one's own creative powers.

If masculinity has been "the most creative cultural force in history", as Camille Paglia suggests, this has not been so simply through the sheer magnificence of men. Women's needs for self-expression, our capacity for introspection, and the value of our own subjectivity have been neglected. The culture has not demanded or expected the creative achievements of women. It demanded creation of men and valued men's philosophies. Few men would feel guilty about locking themselves in a room to write a novel. Few would feel any ambivalence in devoting themselves to a canvas. Even young children will understand that when Daddy is working, he must not be disturbed. There is a sanctity to his creation. It is primary, for man, to have this time and space. He is expected to achieve and create. The act itself justifies the placement of his devotions, and perhaps even obsession.

Few women have had this kind of social space to devote to their interior worlds. Perhaps this is why we have fewer women songwriters than we should have. Perhaps this is why we do not have the numbers of women painters, musicians and writers that we could enjoy. And perhaps this is why feminists who do not have children have been able to produce more chapters on the burdens of motherhood than most feminist mothers ever will. Certainly this is the reason the creative will of women is, in itself and by its very existence, a revolutionary force. And this is also why feminism must include a consciousness of women's needs for creative self-expression – an incorporation of a kind of women's "renaissance".

For me, issues of feminism and creativity converged in a frustration which doubled, multiplied and finally forced me, for my own well-being and survival, to acknowledge the toll extracted from my life by the repression and dissipation of my own creative impulses. From that point, it was essential for me to understand the relatedness of feminist consciousness and creativity. There could be no separation between awareness and expression. Coming to feminist consciousness was not only about realising that I could "be the man" I wanted to marry, or the man I wanted to seduce, but also that I could be the artist I wanted to inspire.

As much as the muse has suggested the profound powers within women, these powers are useless to us until they represent "something we can do, rather than something we have — a verb rather than a noun".[2] I found a fuller life for myself as a writer and as a woman beginning at the same time, and leading me out of the crises of self and "nothingness" in which I had been caught. And so I believe that, among the essential aspects of a more personal feminism, we must include the demystification of our roles in the creative process; a deep focus upon our own creative impulses; and the conviction that inspiration and creation are neither masculine nor feminine, but human.

A recognition of women's own creativity would undoubtedly have its repercussions. It might begin to penetrate familiar life, lifting some of the resentment we have felt, diminishing the importance of the roles we never chose for ourselves, and restoring a measure of naturalism to the home and relationships between partners. Many women never have a relationship with their inner creative selves, partly because the daily demands of life leave us little energy and partly because we have been taught that to reserve any energy for ourselves would be selfish. Others may see our introspection as withdrawing some part of our love for them, but this is not the case. We are not subtracting anything from those around us; we are adding a relationship with ourselves to the mix and becoming more capable of meaningful relationships with others as a result. This is a healthy and essential self-centredness, not selfishness.

And there will be other benefits, beyond our homes and immediate relationships. As we begin to find our own voices, begin to see creative inspiration as part of our human – not feminine – existence, and claim our inspirational powers for ourselves, we will create the realistic images of women that we have lacked, we will see reaffirming images of ourselves reflected in the world we live in, and we will convey this affirmation to generations of daughters who inherit our gifts.

Whatever the convenient, but inequitable, constructions of social life have taken from the human spirit – whatever we have split and dismembered through hyper-rationality – can be put together again by responding to our senses. As Nin suggested, the life of the senses, of feeling and emotion, can lead us back to wholeness, integrity, and to experience of everything in its totality, with the full command of our own powers. And as our work – the expression of our energy – becomes more than what we do to make money or keep households, it becomes a life work. It is what we need to do with our opportunity at living. It is not profit- or power-oriented. It is no less than our connection to the universe. Attaining this sort of "total" or complete existence is not a mechanical process. There are no formulaic solutions to the crises of self.

There were some concrete steps I took towards myself, described in my previous chapter. These exercises were fairly easy to describe, but there was another aspect to this process.

There were other, more abstract mood-setting techniques which helped bring me to a closer connection with my true, inner self. None of this took any special skill, training or therapy, but it took time, concentration, and a desire to find my own means of expression.

Nin suggests that when we have fallen back upon the "pseudo-scientific terminology of psychology" it has been because "we were trained to think in terms of science, since science says you can explore the unconscious very safely. We believed Freud more readily than we believed the poet or mystic... our culture did not prepare us, did not give the poet his status."[3] When we try to speak of exploring the subconscious by way of artistic expression, we are told that we cannot attempt to interpret the meaning or purpose of art. Maybe people just feel that they can't or don't know how to speak of art anymore – perhaps it seems too far away from their daily lives, too removed, too supposedly eccentric, elite, exclusive. Perhaps people don't believe in the power of true expression and communication through art or through anything, or don't witness it enough, or don't attempt it often enough.

The barriers we face – internal and external, real and imagined – are varied. Perhaps the greatest danger is that, having been denied the time and space for an interior life, we might have begun to consider self-expression and creativity almost the exclusive and specialised vocations of some professional cadre of full-time artists, most of them men. But the artist is not simply the one who gives us music or poetry, painting or philosophy. We have all been born to imagine, to create, to express, and to act. The artist is one who is able to show, in any aspect of everyday living, our capacity to restore our own selves, to raise the level of living, and to transform our lives by our own efforts.

Novelist Toni Morrison contends that our grave need to cope with even the harshest realities has always been attended to by artists. In her view, it is part of the artist's role to translate matters of the kind of enormity that cannot be fathomed by the conscious mind. In *Beloved*, Morrison approached the stark reality of slavery not as an historian, but as an artist: examining every one of its cold iron instruments of torture, imagining each event of their implementation, gagging in empathy with her protagonist as she tried to swallow through a muzzle designed to fit inside her mouth, not simply over it. This is the kind of humiliation and degradation of humanity that cannot be conveyed through documentary, but through artistry. It is the kind of reality that cannot be understood at the level of facts, but the level of emotion.[4]

When Morrison initially sat down to write, she was not going to write about slavery. Neither was she going to write a novel. But flashes of imagination – the "unconscious writing" of the artist inside – inspired Morrison to produce the novel she had not intended to write. First to come to her mind was the personality of a woman, then a dynamic of family relationships, and finally the context of slavery. Always, in the truest moments of creation, the emotional realities of human beings – the inner realities – are first and primary. Then there are external circumstances: the trials, the offenses, the degradation of our essence. And then there is a need for re-creation of ourselves and comprehension of the journey – and that, often, is the core of the artist's work and the work of the artist in each of us.

Another barrier to genuine expression is the insecurity and fear of judgment which drives us to censor and edit ourselves, to be stingy with our emotions, to be parsimonious in our revelations. The fears we have are the fears of other human beings, the opinions they will hold, and the criticism they will level at us. But if we have put forward the most honest and truthful aspects of ourselves, the integrity of the work always remains. The deep, genuine, truthful aspects of ourselves are not destructible. At times we might feel hurt by criticism, but our own subjective truths remain undeniable and unshakeable. When Nin needed to imbibe, when she needed to nourish and resurrect herself, she did it through artistic communion: "When I need drugs, when the present is unacceptable, I reread all my French books, saturate myself with the delectable [Jean] Giraudoux, with the poetic analysis of [Pierre Jean] Jouve. Above all, with the certitudes of people who never refused or eluded experience, for whom experience of life was the primary motivation, who were unafraid of love, sex, even madness or evil."[5]

In the same way, when we do not feel able to create – when we feel gripped by fear of our own anxieties and others' judgements – we can turn to the work of other artists and find nourishment, encouragement and a sense of community there. Surrounded by the work of sincere artists, we can feel less alone in speaking a language of emotions and writing of human qualities, without the need for fantastic or romantic elaboration.

Before I started to take account of my feelings through writing, on the verge of my own sort of madness, I thought there would be no way for me to produce words that would speak from my heart and mind in an unconscious, unedited and uncensored way. I thought I would always want to produce the version of myself that I would like people to believe and would make me feel comfortable. Yet I never found enduring comfort in any of the embroidered, embellished or white-washed versions of me. Comfort has come in facing my whole self, including the "shameful" and uncomfortable bits. In other words, comfort has been in acceptance of the truth.

I learned to be truthful about myself by surrounding myself with the work of artists whose honesty shocked me, surprised me and made me want to communicate honestly, too. There are people among us who have worked to develop their own modes of awareness and who can serve as beacons for us. They are not only the sages, saints and prophets who seem to be leagues ahead of us. They are those people who are doing the difficult, tedious, incremental work of the self and its expression. You will know when you come upon artists who write, speak or sing from the heart. You will feel them speak to you from the places which too few of us ever reveal. If you surround yourself with their work, true communication will begin to seem the norm. It was the honesty of artists that helped me find my own voice, and gave me encouragement to speak the language of emotional truths. I have begun to feel part of a larger project, in which the idea of editing myself has become almost impossible and untrue to the work. Fear and worries about others' pronouncements no longer censor me and are never as important as coming close to the truth.

In the safety of a creative environment which I have fashioned for myself, any hesitations I have had only made me more interested and curious to pursue the truth. When I hear songwriter Natalie Merchant call herself "Jezebel", I also have been inspired to find creative ways to look at women's loves, regrets and feelings of being "jaded". Listening to her music, I feel less isolated by my own experiences of life and less alone in my work, even though her medium is very different from mine and is demanding in different ways. I feel part of a community of artists with the same intention to ascertain human truths by revealing and testifying to their own. With the reassuring examples set by other creative selves, I have realised that there are points at which the personal ceases to be simply personal and is profoundly and broadly human. Through analysis, craft and technique, it can even become art. You only need to step back from the narrowness of your own specific and temporal circumstances to begin to appreciate the symbolism of larger processes of growth and struggle. As the support of other artists encouraged me to do just that, my experience has seemed something that is not simply mine, not that of a particularly unusual woman or unlikely events, but essentially a human story of human circumstances.

The creative support I found in a "community of artists" might not exist in many obvious ways. Where I live, there are no artists' enclaves or anything resembling the "cafe society" like that in which Anaïs Nin flourished. But even when we are not around other people who have specific interests in creative self-expression, or when we do not feel able to make contact with such people, we can find support through their work. Nin felt compelled to tell us that when she wrote her first book, on D. H. Lawrence – which propelled her into Parisian literary society – she was living the isolated life of a suburban housewife. She reminded us that while a Parisian suburb might sound exciting to us, a suburb is a suburb: "It is the same loneliness, it's the same isolation. There aren't books enough in the library, and there aren't many people to talk to."[6] Nin had to draw upon the work of Lawrence, Giraudoux and Jouve to form her own creative environment. So however removed or exclusive the artists' world might seem to us, we must realise that a lot of that world is mystique and that the bulk of creative work has never been done in a pub or cafe, but in the many lonely hours during which artists rely upon experiencing their sense of separateness as a creative thing, a source of unique sensibilities. Many artists choose to isolate themselves, in order to focus upon those sensibilities. And so, as women, we need not allow any sense of isolation make us feel excluded from responding to our own creative impulses. Often these impulses themselves bring us beyond our limited worlds. In the meantime, support for our creative impulses can be found and does exist, everywhere and in the most remote parts, in the ways that one artist's dream can foster and nourish another's.

When I am facing a creative block or feeling overwhelmed by the events of my daily routines, I can put on the music of Paul Brady and his insight becomes immediately available to me. A few lines from him can expose the macho emotional distance and romantic illusion which so much of the rest of popular musical culture reinforces. The dream-like quality and poetic expressiveness of "Take Me Away" goes a long way to suggest the excitement and vulnerability of the world of a boy. And while "The Road to the Promised Land" could be heard simply as a romance between a man and a woman, for me it is a song of composites – men, women, and our approaches to life together. Every time I listen to that song, it is easier for

me to envision and believe in the possibility of true communion between men and women. As I listen to the words, I
begin to believe that I am not alone in having and hoping for
that vision. Certainly it helps that Paul Brady is so careful to
describe the scene is detail, with the "dawn tide... turning".
And it also helps that he is steadfast. The journey he describes
is fraught with danger and, from the onset, is denied by others
who caution that "You'll find nothing there." For me, this
song is like a mantra, a secular prayer.

The work of the unconscious is like a many-voiced sym-
phony. It is one of the projects in which the support we can
offer to each other feels something like the truly liberating
ethic of "big love". It is the excitement and verification of
finding your innermost intuitions expressed in the eloquence
of others – a communion of selves which almost defies
description. Like many artists who take on this type of work,
Brady often draws upon the terms of an emotional landscape
to describe the process. The sea, the road, the river are the
recurrent images and motifs for artists attempting to communicate a mystical journey, symbolic of all the ways in which
our conscious and subconscious lives are intertwined. Brady
has said that the point of songwriting, for him, is in "finding
something new... finding something in yourself that you didn't
find before. Singing it is just the fun of it, but it's the actual
writing of it, the digging it up... that brings something new."

Gloria Steinem also spoke of going deep down into herself,
as she related her need to rejuvenate and sustain herself
through writing: "It's like diving for pearls in an ocean of the
unconscious: sometimes you come up with a gem, sometimes
you don't, but either way, you emerge renewed."[7]

Psychoanalyst Ira Progoff used the metaphor of the well in relating our need to find expression of our true selves and communicate with others. He suggested that in "digging down" to find the deepest source of ourselves, we also find a connection in the depths, a connection to the rivers which feed all the wells.[8] This deepest level is that of our collective unconscious – the level of human emotion and feeling.

Just as the greater mass of earth is not evident, a great part of life is dreamed and felt subconsciously. This realm is part of our reality, our emotional reality. Many people refer to having a sense of an "underlying" reality to life, a reality which is a personal source of meaning. Part of the role of the artist, as witness to this realm and its significance, is to divine the words that could describe the connections between our conscious and subconscious lives. The artist – and the artist persona within each of us – understands that we must pursue this relationship in the interests of our own awareness. Each fragment of creative expression might become part of the foundation of a greater sensitivity, with lives lived on the basis and expectation of authentic encounters and sincere relationships.

Artists make it a point to remain aware and sensitive to our most basic, human, subconscious needs. Even when she has felt destroyed by life, the artist has gone about the restoration work that has helped us all to live. She concentrates on the inner world of the subconscious and projects it. She performs the essential role of bringing subconscious sensitivity to conscious life through creativity. Yet, as a society, we often disparage the "artist" for being a kind of temperamental prima donna. We have suggested the work of human creativity is superfluous, non-productive, extravagant and dispensable. We have called the worlds of artists, musicians and writers "elit-ist" and "eccentric", suggesting there is something unnatural or cultist in creative lifestyles. We have resented artists for attempting to find an internal morality and integrity, despite social dictates. But without the moments of reflection and perspective that the artist offers, we might be crushed under the weight of this hyper-rational life.

Nin believed that as the artist taps into the unconscious, she gives us access to the powers of the mind that are constant, yet timeless, and releases us from the friction of daily life. When the artist's work has been disparaged as "a most unvir-tuous thing to do, to escape from the present", Nin defended this world of escape as "a place in which to recover our vision ... a place in which to reconstruct ourselves after shattering experiences."[9]

Nin saw it as the role of the artist to create a more tolera-ble, transformable, livable present. Her journals had helped her cope and carry on when, at the age of eleven, she moved to a country where she did not speak the language and her family became separated. In her diary, she created a small world in which she could cope and confide. Her writing became her stabiliser. It was through her own creativity that she learned to transmute the stultifying moments. Through writing and music she learned to carry on and find suste-nance, even in the midst of "sorrows and war and dissidence, divorce and separation... This is what we must not forget, and which we did when we disparaged the necessity, the indis-pensable quality of art in our lives."[10]

Perhaps the artist knows better than anyone that the world is a subjective creation, a series of choices and selection of elements within which all is possible. It is remarkable that, despite the horrors all around us, many artists continue to choose to dream and depict its opposite. Nin understood the importance of keeping the expressive aspects of our own selves active and aware, despite hardship and through desperate times. She also understood that, not through politics alone, but also by tapping into the depths of our creative selves, we can learn not to despair and will begin to produce the moral, equitable, intelligent society that we need.

In plumbing the depths of unconscious undercurrents, the artist – or "mystic" – uses what is available to all of us: knowledge of previous experience, human qualities of inference and imagination, and the most basic instruments of discovery. We can all see, hear, feel, learn, think and react. Drawing upon our deepest understandings and common senses, we can all attempt to come closer to the essential themes and most basic human concerns of the collective unconscious. With honesty and sincerity, it is within the range of any of us to strike a universal chord, to speak to others, to become relevant, to create moments of identification and to diminish despair through the comfort of companionship and insight.

Now when I look back on times when I felt loneliness and emptiness, I feel a very deep appreciation for those women whose selves are still repressed and denied. This is what a broad feminist consciousness is all about, for me. It is not simply about or for women who have prospects or power. Feminism belongs just as much to women who do not know or speak its name. We must consider, extremely sensitively and lovingly, all of the women who, perhaps lacking self-confidence, have had some creative disturbance and restlessness and may have felt that they had undeveloped potentials. These are the women who, like many of us, are most apt to invest in the people around them the faith that they should have in themselves. Part of our responsibility as feminists is to help such women find the ways to make their silence eloquent.

Nin always emphasised that the writing she accomplished was not the result of some exclusive or exceptional gift: "I want you to know that at twenty I wrote very badly." She gave the original draft of her first novel to the library of Northwestern University (Evanston, Illinois, USA) so that we could see that the artist's work is not simply what we see when the artist attains fame or notoriety. She was quite conscious of the importance of this contribution. Nin believed that it was vitally important, in understanding the creative process and the evolution of artistry, to also understand that at the age of twenty she was "mute". Even at thirty, she listened to other people, but never said a word. She volunteers the fact that she was not even able to speak to the people she knew – and she does all of this in order to emphasise that there was a lot that had to be overcome before she could believe in herself and the value of what she had to say.

Nin is remarkable for having made the development of her own feminist consciousness a life-long project. To me, she was *the* self-made woman. I know that some people will disagree with calling Nin a feminist. In her personal life she was most closely associated with Henry Miller, a "macho" American writer, and in her professional life she was associated with D. H. Lawrence, who is also considered a chauvinist. Her views of male homosexuality are confused and peculiar. Much of the time she does flip-flop between a super-inflated and painfully deflated ego, often falling back upon her charms and beauty. It is impossible not to have difficulty in reconciling these matters with aspects of her insight.

But Nin is not noteworthy for having lived a life of seduction. That, in itself, is not particularly interesting or unusual, though people have chosen to write books on that exclusively. What Nin is remarkable for is in having recognised her patterns of seduction, acknowledged them and analysed them. No one has been better able to articulate the connection between women's self-expression, inner growth and self-worth: "I taught myself to talk, and I owe to writing the fact that we can talk together now." No one more encouraged women – "who have operated on a combination of instinct, emotion, intellect, and observation, a synthesis which we call intuition" – to learn to articulate and become focused in ourselves. Nin, more than anyone else I have come across, has pleaded for the "revelation of woman who is not only trying to be revealed to herself but needs to be revealed to others".[11] This is feminist in the deepest senses.

Insofar as the early, radical roots of the women's movement of the 1960s began with philosophical experiments in women's expression and thought, early feminists might have been influenced by Nin, for whom writing was not simply writing, but something necessary to living and a method of self-orientation. The legacy of the most philosophical strains of feminism is in the discipline of women's studies, which began by asking questions about the omission of women's lives from the historical record and included writing assignments which required students to keep journals and produce "reflection" and "reaction" papers. Setting aside time for such explorations says something about the way we value women's inner lives and affirms the importance and uniqueness of our authentic selves.

It hardly matters whether your method of orientation is writing, or meditation, or therapy, or some other form of reflection or reflective craft. There is no single way of taking the inner journey toward the true aspects of ourselves. The means is not as important as the quest itself – the search for some inner core, some basis for understanding, a capacity for evaluation, and confirmation of the reality of our own selves by, somehow, communicating the truth of our existence. Both Nin and Steinem have emphasised that even the most elementary forms of expressive arts can be as significant as accomplished works, if they help us get closer to our true selves. Both suggest that we can begin to create in "naïve" ways, just as children do: painting with their fingers, picking up a brush as soon as they can hold one; telling stories as soon as they can converse; growing seeds in egg cartons as a prelude to cultivating a garden; modelling clay while dexterity is still only developing.

Indeed, Nin began her novels in a "naïve" way, with "one line which was an image, and I wouldn't even know where I was going from there". In her diary, she would begin each entry with whatever event of the day was the warmest, nearest or strongest one. That was her method of selection, and from that point she would begin to unravel its roots in the past and branches into the future. Often she found that apparently casual occurrences could reveal insights into critical emotional aspects of herself.

Steinem took a very different route, beginning with simple

forms of body relaxation and self-hypnosis, which gradually led to deeper focus upon the unconscious thoughts and creative will she had blocked. It is in these states – when inner focus is sufficiently intense to allow us to engage with our uncensored, unconscious thoughts – that we can work through blocks in conscious thought and begin to produce the work that truly speaks for us. It is from these states that I have found myself writing the things that I have needed to know: what I really thought, what I really felt and what I really wanted.

I once read of a man who carried around a tape recorder for a week, recording every thought he had. At the end of the week, he had 200 pages of text. Most of it was useless, but some of it was interesting. The point of his exercise was to show that, by listening closely enough to our interior monologue, we might extract a few of the messages that will be significant to conscious life. Similarly, Steinem describes a kind of unconscious or "automatic" writing of everything that comes into your head, as it happens, "writing so quickly and in such quantity – as much as is physically possible for a set period of time – that censoring by a critical self becomes simply impossible".[12]

None of this has anything to do with literary skill or external measures of artistic value. And none of it has to please any critics. The point is to reach some part of yourself that you need to recognise. As Cecil Day-Lewis suggested, at our creative best, we are not so much motivated by a need to be understood as by a more personal and urgent need to understand something about ourselves.

Ira Progoff encouraged people to put their minds forward into their wishes by having a dialogue with a dead artist, or even with someone they had never met. Progoff worked with diverse groups of people, including those who could not read or write, and found them all able to articulate vivid dreams, aspirations, wishes and positive steps toward personal fulfilment.

All of this is about learning to articulate our own creative wishes – not the whimsical hopes that we can only dash our heads against, but the self-conscious visions of human potentials – the creation of our futures through artistic and creative controls. This tempered plan – whether written, or dreamed, or created in some other way – can become a kind of blueprint for living more creatively and more humanly; not "the impossible, the absolute thing, the romantic thing, the neurotic thing, the narcissistic thing like trying to find the twin who says 'yes' to everything".[13]

As much as these most human blueprints, these transcending visions, are creative, they are also feminist. They are feminist in acceptance of both the potentials and limitations of human beings, resistance to romanticism, and emphasis upon the importance of claiming and desiring our rights to our own futures. For too long too many of us have defined desire as desire of man. Just as significantly, we have linked desire and romance so closely that we viewed the ability to act on desires as an attribute of man alone: man could desire, woman could only be desired. Woman could not go forward to make her desire real; she had to wait for it. How much more human it is to desire many creative wishes for the multiple facets of ourselves. Then, even when love disappoints us and romance proves to be an illusion, we will know that our futures can be fulfilled independently of men. We will know that a diversity of wishes will sustain us and help us persevere.

Notes

လ

The Culture of Romance

1. Judith Stacey, "The New Conservative Feminism," *Feminist Studies*, vol. 7, no. 3, Fall 1983, p. 576.
2. Adrienne Rich, "Women and Honour: Some Notes on Lying (1975)," *On Lies, Secrets and Silence: Selected Prose 1966-1978*, W.W. Norton 1979, p. 190.
3. Gloria Steinem, *Outrageous Acts and Everyday Rebellions*, Holt, Rinehart and Winston 1983, pp. 19-10.

The Culture of Romance

1. Robert A. Johnson, *We: Understanding the Psychology of Romantic Love*, Harper 1983, p. 48.
2. Ibid. p. xv.
3. Adrienne Rich, "Compulsive Heterosexuality and Lesbian Experience," *Signs: Journal of Women in Culture and Society*, Vol. 4 (Summer 1980), p. 648.
4. Johnson, *We: Understanding the Psychology of Romantic Love*, p. 47.
5. Dorothy C. Holland and Margaret A. Eisenhart, *Educated in Romance*, University of Chicago Press 1990, p. 93.
6. Erich Fromm, *The Art of Loving*, Unwin 1984, p. 10.
7. Holland and Eisenhart, *Educated in Romance*, p. 122.
8. Ibid., p. 121.
9. Ibid., pp. 216-225.
10. Ibid., p. 203.
11. Sharon Thompson, "Search for Tomorrow: On Feminism and the Reconstruction of Teen Romance," in Carol S. Vance (ed), *Pleasure and Danger: Exploring Female Sexuality*, Routledge 1984, pp. 354-360.

12. See Mirra Komarovsky, *Blue-Collar Marriage*, Vintage/Random House 1967; Lillian Rubin, *Worlds of Pain*, Basic Books 1976; Jessie Bernard, *The Future of Marriage*, Bantam 1973.
13. For a man's perspective on the changes that have occurred in expectations and standards for relationships, see Warren Farrell, *The Myth of Male Power*, Hamish Hamilton 1994.
14. Anne Wilson Schaef, *Women's Reality*, Winston Press 1981, p. 108.
15. Gloria Steinem, *Revolution from Within: A Book of Self-Esteem*, Corgi Books 1993, p. 312.
16. Bernard, *The Future of Marriage*, pp. 29-32.
17. Rochelle Gatlin, *American Women Since 1945*, Macmillan Educational 1987, p. 57.
18. Anaïs Nin, *The Journals of Anaïs Nin,* Vol. 4, Quartet Books 1974, p. 137.
19. Adrienne Rich in Barbara Charlesworth Gelpi and Albert Gelpi (eds) *Adrienne Rich's Poetry*, W.W. Norton 1975, p. 95.
20. Sylvia Plath, *The Bell Jar*, Bantam 1972, p. 69.
21. Adrienne Rich, *Of Woman Born: Motherhood as Experience and Institution*, W.W. Norton 1976, pp. 277, 279.
22. Madonna Kolbenschlag, *Goodbye Sleeping Beauty: Breaking the Spell of Feminine Myths and Models*, Arlen House/The Women's Press 1983, p. 179.

Into the Labyrinth

1. *The Gerry Ryan Show*, produced by Joan Torsney, Radio Telefis Eireann, 22 November 1993.
2. Gloria Steinem, "Why Young Women Are More Conservative," *Outrageous Acts and Everyday Rebellions,* Holt, Rinehart and Winston 1983, pp. 211-218.
3. Dorothy C. Holland and Margaret A. Eisenhart, *Educated in Romance*, University of Chicago Press 1990, p. 144.
4. Ibid., p. 145.
5. Ibid., p. 146.
6. Gloria Steinem, *Revolution From Within: A Book of Self-Esteem,* Corgi 1993, p. 48.
7. Ibid., p. 321.
8. Robert A. Johnson, *We: Understanding the Psychology of Romantic Love*, Harper 1983, p. 171.

The Cult of Man's Love
1. Anaïs Nin, *Henry and June*, Penguin 1990, pp. 125-126.
2. Gloria Steinem, *Revolution From Within: A Book of Self-Esteem*, Corgi 1993, p. 312.
3. Anaïs Nin in Evelyn J. Hinz (ed), *A Woman Speaks: The Lectures, Seminars and Interviews of Anaïs Nin*, Penguin 1992, p. 89.
4. Steinem, *Revolution From Within*, pp. 301-302.
5. Nin, *Henry and June*, pp. 172, 178.
6. Ibid., p. 178.
7. Ibid.
8. Ibid., p. 148, p. 162, p. 178.
9. Ibid., p. 182, p. 183.
10. Hinz, *A Woman Speaks*, p. 35.
11. Anaïs Nin, *The Early Diary of Anaïs Nin, Volume Four*, Quartet Books 1974, p. 35.
12. Steinem, *Revolution From Within*, p. 312.

The Usual Poses
1. Gloria Steinem, *Revolution From Within: A Book of Self-Esteem*, Corgi 1993, pp. 324-325.
2. Ibid., p. 325.
3. Nancy Chodorow, *The Reproduction of Mothering: Psychoanalysis and the Sociology of Gender*, University of California Press 1978, p. 214.
4. See Betty Briedan, *The Feminine Mystique*, Dell 1974.
5. Gloria Steinem, *Outrageous Acts and Everyday Rebellions*, Holt, Reinhart and Winston 1983, pp. 212-213.
6. A view considered by Eileen Battersby, "Exasperated Voice of Common Sense," *The Irish Times*, 13 January 1994, p. 13.
7. See Katie Roiphe, *The Morning After: Sex, Fear and Feminism*, Hamish Hamilton 1994; Camille Paglia, *Sexual Personae*, Penguin 1993; Naomi Wolf, *Fire With Fire: The New Female Power and How It Will Change the 21st century*, Hamish Hamilton 1993. And for a consideration of the "diagnostic" bend of such political analyses, see Gloria Steinem, *Outrageous Acts and Everyday Rebellions*, p. 174.
8. Philip Slater in Rochelle Gatlin, *American Women Since 1945*, Macmillan Educational 1987, p. 99.
9. Anaïs Nin, *Henry and June*, Penguin 1990, pp. 125-126.

10. Ibid., pp. 114, 139.
11. Ibid., pp. 142, 145.
12. Adrienne Rich, *Of Woman Born: Motherhood as Experience and Institution*, W.W. Norton 1976, p. 68.
13. Anaïs Nin, *The Early Diary of Anaïs Nin*, Vol. 4, Harvest/Harcourt Brace Jovanovich 1986, p. 37, p. 134.
14. Anaïs Nin, *The Journals of Anaïs Nin*, Vol. 4, Quartet Books 1976, p. 111.
15. Adrienne Rich, "Women and Honor: Some Notes on Lying," *On Lies, Secrets and Silence: Selected Prose*, 1966–1978, W.W. Norton 1979, p. 190.

The Self-Made Woman

1. Gloria Steinem, *Revolution From Within: A Book of Self-Esteem,* Corgi 1993, p. 35.
2. Ibid., p. 13.
3. Adrienne Rich, *Of Woman Born: Motherhood as Experience and Institution,* W.W. Norton 1976, p. 16.
4. Rochelle Gatlin, *American Women Since 1945,* Macmillan Educational 1987, p. 120.
5. Gloria Steinem, interview on *The Phil Donahue Show,* New York: National Broadcasting Company, 1993.
6. For detailed discussion see Gatlin, "Women in Political Movements of the 1960s," *American Women Since 1945*, p. 120.
7. Anaïs Nin, *In Favour of the Sensitive Man,* Penguin 1992, p. 25.
8. Anaïs Nin in Evelyn J. Hinz (ed), *A Woman Speaks: The Lectures, Seminars and Interviews of Anaïs Nin,* Penguin 1992, p. 80.
9. Chrissy Iley, "Something to Shout About," *Sunday Times,* 16 January 1994, p. 4.
10. Steinem, *Revolution From Within*, p. 183.
11. Sylvia Plath in Janet Malcolm, "The Silent Woman I," *New Yorker*, 23 and 30 August 1993, p. 97.
12. Steinem, *Revolution From Within*, p. 228.
13. Nin, *A Woman Speaks*, pp. 172–173.
14. Gatlin, *American Women Since 1945*, p. 76.
15. Ibid., p. 260.
16. Nin, *A Woman Speaks*, p. 213.

17. Steinem, *Revolution From Within*, p. 151.
18. Ibid.
19. Ibid., p. 144.
20. Robert A. Johnson, *We: Understanding the Psychology of Romantic Love,* Harper 1983, pp. 76-77.

Reinventing Womanhood
 1. Gloria Steinem, *Revolution From Within: A Book of Self-Esteem*, Corgi 1993, p. 139.
 2. Ibid., pp. 12-14.
 3. Gloria Steinem, *Outrageous Acts and Everyday Rebellions*, Holt, Rinehart and Winston 1983, p. 174.
 4. Rochelle Gatlin, *American Women Since 1945*, Macmillan Educational 1987, pp. 207-211.
 5. Steinem, *Outrageous Acts and Everyday Rebellions*, pp. 170-171; Betty Friedan, *The Feminine Mystique*: Dell Publishing 1974, p. 333.
 6. Gatlin, *American Women Since 1945*, pp. 47-48.
 7. Ibid., pp. 77-114.
 8. "Developments in Women's Rights," Encarta, Microsoft, 1995.
 9. Ibid., pp. 196, 206.
10. Ibid., pp. 25, 30, 196.
11. Ibid., p. 47.
12. Steinem, *Outrageous Acts and Everyday Rebellions*, p. 172.
13. Louise Knapp Howe, *Pink Collar Workers: Inside the World of Women's Work*, Avon Books 1978, p. 234.
14. Madonna Kolbenschlag, *Goodbye Sleeping Beauty: Breaking the Spell of Feminine Myths and Models*, Arlen House/The Women's Press 1983, p. 92.
15. Gatlin, *American Women Since 1945*, p. 76.
16. Ibid., p. 260.

Mothers of Invention
 1. Adrienne Rich in Barbara Charlesworth Gelpi and Albert Gelpi (eds), *Adrienne Rich's Poetry*, W.W. Norton 1975, p. 95.
 2. Adrienne Rich in Kirsten Grimstad and Susan Rennie (eds), *The New Woman's Survival Sourcebook*, Alfred A. Knopf 1975, p. 110.
 3. Edith M. Stein, "Women are Household Slaves," in Aileen

S. Kraditor (ed), *Up From the Pedestal: Selected Writings in the History of American Feminism,* Quadrangle 1970, p. 352.

4. Anthea McTiernan, "Just More Female Mud-Wrestling," *The Irish Times,* 13 January 1994, p. 13.

5. Ibid.

6. Madonna Kolbenschlag, *Goodbye Sleeping Beauty: Breaking the Spell of Feminine Myths and Models,* Arlen House/The Women's Press 1983, p. 48.

7. Gloria Steinem, *Revolution From Within: A Book of Self-Esteem,* Corgi 1993, p. 275.

8. Adrienne Rich, *Of Woman Born: Motherhood as Experience and Institution,* W.W. Norton 1976, pp. 225-226.

9. Judy Chicago, *Through the Flower: My Struggle as a Woman Artist,* Anchor/Doubleday 1977, p. 79.

10. Feodor Dostoyevsky in Kolbenschlag, *Goodbye Sleeping Beauty: Breaking the Spell of Feminine Myths and Models,* p. 176.

Consciousness and Creation

1. Gloria Steinem, *Revolution From Within: A Book of Self-Esteem,* Corgi 1993, p. 325.

2. Rochelle Gatlin, *American Women Since 1945,* Macmillan Educational 1987, p. 164.

3. Anaïs Nin in Evelyn J. Hinz (ed), *A Woman Speaks: The Lectures, Seminars and Interviews of Anaïs Nin,* Penguin 1992, pp. 111-112.

4. See Toni Morrison, *Beloved: A Novel,* Picador 1988.

5. Anaïs Nin, *The Journals of Anaïs Nin,* Vol. 5, Quartet Books 1976, p. 46.

6. Nin, *A Woman Speaks,* p. 212.

7. Steinem, *Revolution From Within,* pp. 187-188.

8. See Ira Progoff, *At a Journal Workshop: The Basic Text Guide and Guide for Using the Intensive Journal,* Dialogue House Library 1975.

9. Nin, *A Woman Speaks,* p. 171.

10. Ibid., pp. 172-173.

11. Ibid., p. 76.

12. Steinem, *Revolution From Within,* p. 197.

13. Ibid., p. 118.